S E R I E S

A life-changing encounter
with God's Word from the book of

GALATIANS

ASK DANIEL
FOR ESCALATED
PRINS

NAVPRESS
Discipleship Inside Out®

NAVPRESS○
Discipleship Inside Out®

NavPress is the publishing ministry of The Navigators, an internatior
Christian organization and leader in personal spiritual developme
NavPress is committed to helping people grow spiritually and enjoy liv
of meaning and hope through personal and group resources that a
biblically rooted, culturally relevant, and highly practical.

For a free catalog go to www.NavPress.com

ISBN 978-0-89109-562-0

CONTENTS

ACKNOWLEDGMENTS

The LifeChange series has been produced through the coordinated efforts of a team of Navigator Bible study developers and NavPress editorial staff, along with a nationwide network of field-testers.

Series Editor: Karen Lee-Thorp

HOW TO USE THIS STUDY

Objectives

Most guides in the LifeChange series of Bible studies cover one book of the Bible. Although the LifeChange guides vary with the books they explore, they share some common goals:

1. To provide you with a firm foundation of understanding and a thirst to return to the book.

2. To teach you by example how to study a book of the Bible without structured guides.

3. To give you all the historical background, word definitions, and explanatory notes you need, so that your only other reference is the Bible.

4. To help you grasp the message of the book as a whole.

5. To teach you how to let God's Word transform you into Christ's image.

Each lesson in this study is designed to take 60 to 90 minutes to complete on your own. The guide is based on the assumption that you are completing one lesson per week, but if time is limited you can do half a lesson per week or whatever amount allows you to be thorough.

Flexibility

LifeChange guides are flexible, allowing you to adjust the quantity and depth of your study to meet your individual needs. The guide offers many optional questions in addition to the regular numbered questions. The optional questions, which appear in the margins of the study pages, include the following:

Optional Application. Nearly all application questions are optional; we hope you will do as many as you can without overcommitting yourself.

For Thought and Discussion. Beginning Bible students should be able to handle these, but even advanced students need to think about them. These questions frequently deal with ethical issues and other biblical principles. They often offer cross-references to spark thought, but the references do not give obvious answers. They are good for group discussions.

For Further Study. These include: (a) cross-references that shed light on a topic the book discusses, and (b) questions that delve deeper into the passage. You can omit them to shorten a lesson without missing a major point of the passage.

If you are meeting in a group, decide together which optional questions to prepare for each lesson, and how much of the lesson you will cover at the next meeting. Normally, the group leader should make this decision, but you might let each member choose his or her own application questions.

As you grow in your walk with God, you will find the LIFECHANGE guide growing with you—a helpful reference on a topic, a continuing challenge for application, a source of questions for many levels of growth.

Overview and details

The study begins with an overview of Galatians. The key to interpretation is context—what is the whole passage or book *about?*—and the key to context is purpose—what is the author's *aim* for the whole work? In lesson 1 you will lay the foundation for your study of Galatians by asking yourself, *Why did the author (and God) write the book? What did they want to accomplish? What is the book about?*

In lessons 2 through 11, you will analyze successive passages of Galatians in detail. Thinking about how a paragraph fits into the overall goal of the book will help you to see its purpose. Its purpose will help you see its meaning. Frequently reviewing a chart or outline of the book will enable you to make these connections.

In lesson 12, you will review Galatians, returning to the big picture to see whether your view of it has changed after closer study. Review will also strengthen your grasp of major issues and give you an idea of how you have grown from your study.

Kinds of questions

Bible study on your own—without a structured guide—follows a progression. First you observe: What does the passage *say?* Then you interpret: What does the passage *mean?* Lastly you apply: How does this truth *affect* my life?

Some of the "how" and "why" questions will take some creative thinking, even prayer, to answer. Some are opinion questions without clear-cut right answers; these will lend themselves to discussions and side studies.

Don't let your study become an exercise in knowledge alone. Treat the passage as God's Word, and stay in dialogue with Him as you study. Pray,

"Lord, what do You want me to see here?" "Father, why is this true?" "Lord, how does this apply to my life?"

It is important that you write down your answers. The act of writing clarifies your thinking and helps you to remember.

Study aids

A list of reference materials, including a few notes of explanation to help you make good use of them, begins on page 133. This guide is designed to include enough background to let you interpret with just your Bible and the guide. Still, if you want more information on a subject or want to study a book on your own, try the references listed.

Scripture versions

Unless otherwise indicated, the Bible quotations in this guide are from the New International Version of the Bible. Other versions cited are the Revised Standard Version (RSV), the New American Standard Bible (NASB), and the King James Version (KJV).

Use any translation you like for study, preferably more than one. A paraphrase such as The Living Bible is not accurate enough for study, but it can be helpful for comparison or devotional reading.

Memorizing and meditating

A psalmist wrote, "I have hidden your word in my heart that I might not sin against you" (Psalm 119:11). If you write down a verse or passage that challenges or encourages you and reflect on it often for a week or more, you will find it beginning to affect your motives and actions. We forget quickly what we read once; we remember what we ponder.

When you find a significant verse or passage, you might copy it onto a card to keep with you. Set aside five minutes during each day just to think about what the passage might mean in your life. Recite it over to yourself, exploring its meaning. Then, return to your passage as often as you can during your day, for a brief review. You will soon find it coming to mind spontaneously.

For group study

A group of four to ten people allows the richest discussions, but you can adapt this guide for other sized groups. It will suit a wide range of group types, such as home Bible studies, growth groups, youth groups, and businessmen's studies. Both new and experienced Bible students, and new and mature Christians, will benefit from the guide. You can omit or leave for later years any questions you find too easy or too hard.

The guide is intended to lead a group through one lesson per week. However, feel free to split lessons if you want to discuss them more thoroughly. Or, omit some questions in a lesson if preparation or discussion time is limited. You can always return to this guide for personal study later. You will be able to discuss only a few questions at length, so choose some for discussion and others for background. Make time at each discussion for members to ask about anything they didn't understand.

Each lesson in the guide ends with a section called "For the group." These sections give advice on how to focus a discussion, how you might apply the lesson in your group, how you might shorten a lesson, and so on. The group leader should read each "For the group" at least a week ahead so that he or she can tell the group how to prepare for the next lesson.

Each member should prepare for a meeting by writing answers for all of the background and discussion questions to be covered. If the group decides not to take an hour per week for private preparation, then expect to take at least two meetings per lesson to work through the questions. Application will be very difficult, however, without private thought and prayer.

Two reasons for studying in a group are accountability and support. When each member commits in front of the rest to seek growth in an area of life, you can pray with one another, listen jointly for God's guidance, help one another to resist temptation, assure each other that the other's growth matters to you, use the group to practice spiritual principles, and so on. Pray about one another's commitments and needs at most meetings. Spend the first few minutes of each meeting sharing any results from applications prompted by previous lessons. Then discuss new applications toward the end of the meeting. Follow such sharing with prayer for these and other needs.

If you write down each other's applications and prayer requests, you are more likely to remember to pray for them during the week, ask about them at the next meeting, and notice answered prayers. You might want to get a notebook for prayer requests and discussion notes.

Notes taken during discussion will help you to remember, follow up on ideas, stay on the subject, and clarify a total view of an issue. But don't let note-taking keep you from participating. Some groups choose one member at each meeting to take notes. Then someone copies the notes and distributes them at the next meeting. Rotating these tasks can help include people. Some groups have someone take notes on a large pad of paper or erasable marker board so that everyone can see what has been recorded.

Page 136 lists some good sources of counsel for leading group studies.

HISTORICAL BACKGROUND
Paul and Galatia

Map of Paul's Missionary Journey

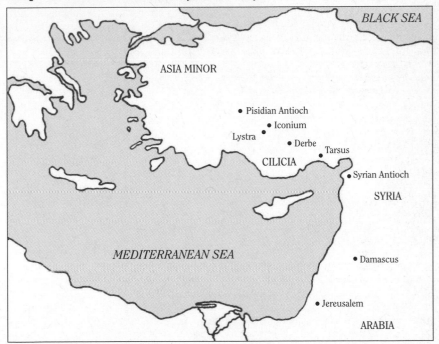

The early church

Just before the risen Christ returned to heaven, He instructed His disciples, "But you will receive power when the Holy Spirit comes on you; and you will be my witnesses in Jerusalem, and in all Judea and Samaria, and to the ends of the earth" (Acts 1:8). The early believers boldly proclaimed Jesus Christ as eternal Lord and Savior, the fulfillment of all God had promised for His chosen people Israel. Thousands in Jerusalem responded to their proclamation (see Acts 2:41).

Major Events of Paul's Life and Ministry

	SUGGESTED DATES[1]
Birth at Tarsus in Cilicia (Acts 21:39; 22:3)	?
Training in Jerusalem (Acts 22:3; 26:4-5)	?
Persecution of Early Church (Acts 8:1-3; 9:1-2; 22:45; 26:9-11)	?
Conversion (Acts 9:3-19; 22:6-16; 26:12-18)	AD 33
Time in Arabia, Damascus (Acts 9:19-25; 2 Corinthians 11:31-33; Galatians 1:17)	33-35
Visit to Jerusalem (Acts 9:26-29; Galatians 1:18)	35
Return to Tarsus (Acts 9:30)	35
Teaching at Antioch in Syria (Acts 11:25-26)	45–47
Taking Famine Relief to Jerusalem (Acts 11:27-30; 12:25)	46
First Missionary Journey (Acts 13:1–14:26)	ca. 47–48
Ministry in Antioch (Acts 14:26-28; 15:35)	48–49
Jerusalem Council (Acts 15:1-29)	49
Second Missionary Journey (Acts 15:36–18:22)	ca. 49–52
Third Missionary Journey (Acts 18:23–21:17)	53–57
Arrest at Jerusalem (Acts 21:27–23:22)	57
Imprisonment at Caesarea (Acts 23:23–26:32)	57–59
Transfer to Rome (Acts 27:1–28:15)	59–60
House Arrest in Rome (Acts 28:16-31)	60–62
Release and Further Travels (?) (Titus 1:5; 3:12; 1 Timothy 1:3; 3:14; 2 Timothy 4:13,20; Romans 15:24,28)	62–65?
Final Imprisonment and Death in Rome (2 Timothy 1:16-17; 4:6-8,16-18	65?

When persecution by the Jewish authorities scattered them from Jerusalem, their "good news," the gospel, scattered with them. Still, they only spoke to those who had already embraced the Jewish faith. Non-Jewish people—the Gentiles—were avoided as impure until God Himself showed that they too were now part of His chosen people (see Acts 10:28,34-35; 11:19). Churches with Jews and Gentiles meeting together soon appeared throughout the Roman Empire and beyond. Within forty years, Gentile urban centers had replaced Israel as the focal point of the church.

The apostle Paul

This rapid expansion and extreme diversity brought many moments of confusion and crisis to the early church. God prepared and called a special man to help His Church cross the threshold with its faith and vigor intact.

Paul (then Saul) was born into a family with Roman citizenship and devout Jewish beliefs. His home was in Tarsus, the capital of Cilicia and a city noted as a center of Greek learning. Paul was multilingual and exposed to Greek thought, but he was trained in Jerusalem under Gamaliel, the most respected Jewish teacher of the day. Paul rose to prominence among the Pharisees as one wholly devoted to the detailed observance of God's Law.

Paul's zeal led him to persecute the church for its departure from Jewish traditions. His vision took him far beyond Jerusalem in that mission. One day as Paul traveled toward Damascus with murderous intents against the believers, the glorified Christ confronted him. "Last of all, as if to one born abnormally late, He appeared to me!" (1 Corinthians 15:8, PH). Shaken to the core, the persecutor became a suffering apostle of the truth he once hated.

God specifically called Paul to be an apostle to the Gentiles. Though his heart ached for his fellow Israelites (see Romans 9:1-4; 10:1), his greatest fruit was among other peoples (see Acts 9:15; 22:18,21). His first major period of ministry took place at Antioch in Syria under the discipling of Barnabas. Then God thrust the two men out on a missionary journey (see the Map of Paul's Missionary Journey) that included the establishment of churches in the southern portion of the province of Galatia.

The Galatians

About 280 BC, a group of Celtic warrior tribes known as Galatians established themselves in north-central Asia Minor. They later became a kingdom subject to Rome. When their king died in 25 BC, a Roman province by their name was established. Since the Galatians had ruled over other groups, the Roman province of Galatia included areas south of the original territory.

Paul's first missionary journey (about AD 47) took him into the southern portion of the Galatian province. Churches were established in Pisidian Antioch,[2] Iconium, Lystra, and Derbe (see Acts 13:3–14:23). Many commentators believe these churches were the recipients of Paul's letter to the Galatians.

11

Others think that Paul also visited the original ethnic group in the north, and that these were the people he addressed as Galatians. While nothing in Scripture rules out a visit to northern Galatia, there is no certain record of it. On the other hand, the New Testament is clear regarding Paul's close ties with the southern part of the province (see Acts 16:1-5; 20:4).[3]

The Judaizers

There were many who wanted to twist the early advances of the gospel to their own ends. They would follow Paul and other missionaries, attempting to "straighten out" the new converts to their own crooked ways of thinking (see Galatians 5:7). We call one such group "the Judaizers" because they wanted to Judaize the believers — to make them Jews as well as Gentiles. They taught Gentile converts that "Unless you are circumcised, according to the custom taught by Moses, you cannot be saved" (Acts 15:1; compare Galatians 6:12). They apparently claimed to represent the church leadership in Jerusalem (see Acts 15:24), so some Gentiles obediently began trying to follow the Law (see Galatians 3:2-3; 4:10).

The Law and many traditions were not evil in themselves. Circumcision, dietary restrictions, and special days were within the Christian's liberty to observe (see Acts 16:3; Romans 14:5). Jesus Christ had lived perfectly in the will of the Father as a Jew. Paul himself was a Jew, and Christianity did not require him to abandon his Jewishness in areas unopposed to the truth of the gospel (see Acts 21:20-25; 1 Corinthians 9:20).

But if even Jews looked to the Law as a means to secure God's favor, then their faith was not in Christ and His completed work on the Cross. If the Gentiles were required to practice the Law — an impossible task — then suddenly the means of both salvation and living the Christian life became human effort, rather than faith in God.

Paul's letters

Paul was certainly at the forefront of the expansion in the early Church. Yet many whom the Holy Spirit gifted were boldly spreading the gospel throughout the Roman Empire and beyond. What set Paul apart as a proclaimer and defender of the truth were his letters to the infant churches. They were soon recognized by the church as Scripture inspired by the Holy Spirit (see 2 Peter 3:15-16). Over the centuries, these thirteen[4] letters of the New Testament have repeatedly restored the church to life and teaching in accord with God's truth.

Paul's letter to the Galatians is probably his sternest defense against false teaching. He normally begins each letter with some expression of praise and thankfulness for the faith of his readers. To the Galatians he gives not one word of commendation before he plunges into his counterattack against the inroads of the Judaizers. Like a parent for his children, he bares his heart in an effort to steer his converts in the truth (see Galatians 4:19).

It is possible that Galatians is Paul's earliest epistle.[5] Those who see it as addressed to southern Galatia usually date it in the vicinity of the Jerusalem council of Acts 15 (about AD 48). This meeting of church leaders dealt with the same issues the Galatians faced and involved the same people, if not the same events, that the letter refers to.

The outcome

What resulted from Paul's appeal to the Galatians? Paul was confident that the Galatians would respond to his admonitions (see Galatians 5:10), and we have no indication that it happened otherwise. Paul continued to teach those churches (see Acts 16:14; 18:23). They shared in his collection for the poor believers in Judea (see 1 Corinthians 16:1-2) and provided two of his faithful coworkers (see Acts 16:1; 20:4).

The Judaizers did not fare as well. The Jerusalem council removed from them any pretense of apostolic authority (see Acts 15:1-29). It recognized Gentile believers as having full rights in the Body of Christ without submitting to Jewish requirements. Judaizing efforts weakened, and with the destruction of Jerusalem in AD 70, the church's center shifted to Antioch in Syria. The danger of a church bound to Jewish legalism was past.

1. F. F. Bruce, *The Letters of Paul: An Expanded Paraphrase* (Grand Rapids, MI: Eerdmans, 1965), 8.
2. Pisidian Antioch should not be confused with Syrian Antioch, Paul's sending church. Seleucus Nicator, the general who took over a large section of Alexander the Great's empire after Alexander's death, had a father named Antiochus. Seleucus named sixteen cities after his father.
3. For a complete discussion of the north Galatian and south Galatian views, see Donald Guthrie, *Galatians* (Grand Rapids, MI: Eerdmans, 1973), 15–27. Many other commentaries also address this issue in detail.
4. A few commentators attribute the anonymous book of Hebrews to Paul, which would make the total fourteen.
5. F. F. Bruce, *The Epistle to the Galatians* (Grand Rapids, MI: Eerdmans, 1982), 55.

OVERVIEW AND GALATIANS 1:1-9

The True Gospel

Background

If you have not done so already, read the historical background. Then read through the whole book of Galatians. It is a fairly short letter, and you are just reading for an overall view. If you've read it before, try to get a fresh perspective. As you read, or afterward, jot notes to question 1.

1. Repetition is a clue to the ideas an author wants to emphasize. What key words and phrases occur repeatedly in this letter?

   _____

   _____

   _____

   _____

   _____

   _____

2. According to Galatians 1:7-8, how would you explain the circumstances that led Paul to write this letter?

   _____

   _____

   _____

For Thought and Discussion: Rebuke as strong as Paul gives in this letter is hard to take. What do you think should have made the Galatians want to accept what Paul had to say?

For Thought and Discussion: Why do you think Paul reacted so strongly to the Judaizers?

_____

_____

_____

3. Describe Paul's relationship with and feelings for the Galatian believers in the following verses:

4:11 _____

_____

4:13-15 _____

_____

4:19-20 _____

_____

4. How does he portray the Galatians in the following verses?

1:7 _____

3:1 _____

4:15-16 _____

5:7 _____

5:15 _____

5. What seems to be Paul's mood or tone in this letter?

_____

_____

_____

6. What would you say is the basic purpose of this letter?

_____

_____

_____

_____

_____

7. An outline can help you see how the parts of a
   book relate to each other. In an overview, it's
   helpful just to give titles to the main sections
   of the book. Skim back through Galatians, and
   make up a title for each section listed below.
   Use a short phrase or sentence that summarizes
   the section and distinguishes it from other
   sections. Key words from the section are often
   good in titles.

   1:1-9 _____

   _____

   1:10–2:21 _____

   _____

   _____

   3:1–4:31 _____

   _____

   _____

   5:1 6:10 _____

   _____

   _____

   _____

8. Write down any questions that your first reading of Galatians has raised. They can serve as
   some personal objectives for further study.

   _____

   _____

   _____

   _____

   _____

For Thought and Discussion:
   a. Note by whom and for whom the letter was written (see 1:1-2). How did Paul view himself?
   b. Why do you think Paul introduced himself the way he did in this letter? Consider the situation he was facing.

For Thought and Discussion: List as many features of the gospel message as you can find in 1:1-5. Why do you think Paul incorporated this into his greeting? What lessons can you draw for your own conversation and correspondence?

Greetings (1:1-5)

Apostle (1:1). Literally, a "sent one," one who is appointed and empowered for a specific mission. The term was used of many in the early church designated to spread the gospel (see Acts 14:14; Romans 16:7). In a strict sense it referred to the Twelve, whom Christ Himself chose to bear witness to His teaching and resurrection (see Mark 3:13-15).

   Ancient letters normally begin by identifying the sender and recipient. Paul varied his identifications to suit the situation of the particular letter.

Grace and peace (1:3). A Greek letter normally followed the identifications with a greeting. Paul devised a greeting that invited God's favor and blessing in the broadest terms. "They summarize Paul's gospel of salvation. The nature of salvation is peace, or reconciliation—peace with God, peace with men, peace within. The source of salvation is grace, God's free favour, irrespective of any human merit or works, His lovingkindness to the undeserving."[1]

9. What do you think God's purposes are in rescuing us from "the present evil age" (1:4)? (*Optional:* See Ephesians 1:6,10; 2:4; 3:10-11.)

_____

_____

_____

_____

A different gospel (1:6-9)

Gospel (1:6). Literally, "good news," the message God entrusted to Paul to preach and defend (see 1:12; 2:5,7). "The gospel is the joyous proclamation of God's redemptive activity in Christ Jesus on behalf of men enslaved by sin."[2]

10. From 1:6-9, how do you think Paul would respond to the idea that there are many roads leading to heaven?

_____

_____

_____

_____

_____

For Thought and Discussion: Can you think of some modern perversions of the gospel? How can one discern what is really true and avoid being led astray?

Study Skill — Application

James 1:22 says, "Do not merely listen to the word, and so deceive yourselves. Do what it says." In other words, application is an essential part of Bible study. Every lesson of this study contains both "Optional Applications" in the margins and at least one open-ended application question after the interpretation questions. Application will often require some time for thought, prayer, planning, and action. You may want to discuss the passage with someone else to help you decide how to apply it. You'll be looking for specific ways to do what God's Word says.

Some questions to ask yourself are, "What difference should this passage make to my life? How should it make me want to think or act?" At times, you may find it most productive to concentrate on one application, giving it careful thought, prayer, and effort during the week. At other times, you may want to list many implications a passage has for your life, plan to memorize and meditate on the passage during the week, and look for ways to apply it. Choose whatever strategy is most fruitful.

Don't neglect prayer. As John 15:1-5 points out, you can't do what the Word says unless you are living intimately with Christ and drawing on His power. Go to God for guidance about what to apply and how, for strength to do what He says, for forgiveness when you fail, and for thanksgiving when you succeed.

19

11. What are some things you would like to see happen in your life during your study of Galatians? Write them down, then ask God to accomplish them.

-FREEDOM FROM LEGALISM

- FREEDOM FROM PAST EVENTS

THAT CAUSE ME HATE AND

ANGER

- MORE BONDING W/ FREINDS/ MORE

FRIENDS

CONTINUATION
FROM OF RETREAT
THEME

TRUE FORGIVENESS

For the group

This "For the group" section and the ones in later lessons are intended to suggest ways of structuring your discussions. Feel free to select what suits your group and ignore the rest. The main goals of this lesson are to get to know Galatians as a whole and the people with whom you are going to study it.

Worship. Some groups like to begin with prayer and/or singing. Some share requests for prayer at the beginning, but leave the actual prayer until after the study. Others prefer just to chat and have refreshments for a while and then move to the study, leaving worship until the end. It is a good idea to start with at least a brief prayer for the Holy Spirit's guidance and some silence to help everyone change focus from the day's busyness to the Scripture.

Chart of Galatians

Theme: The Gospel of Freedom in Christ

TRUTH Chapters 1–2	Paul defends his gospel message against perversions that followed.	1:1-9	The Gospel Must Be Kept Pure
		1:10-24	Paul's Gospel Came from God, Not Man
		2:1-10	The Apostles Recognized Paul's Ministry
		2:11-21	Even Peter Needed Paul's Correction
FAITH Chapters 3–4	Relationship with God is based on faith, not on following the law.	3:1-14	Faith Has Always Done What the Law Could Not
		3:15-25	Law Never Replaced God's Promises
		3:26–4:11	In Christ We Are Sons and Heirs, Not Slaves
		4:12-31	Like Isaac, We Are Born for Freedom
SPIRIT Chapters 5–6	Christian living is to be directed by the Spirit, not by the flesh.	5:1-15	God Wants Us Free to Live By Love
		5:16-26	Only the Spirit Can Help Us Overcome the Sinful Nature
		6:1-10	Spiritual Living Is an Ongoing, Group Pursuit
		6:11-18	Internal Change Is Important, Not External Rituals

SPECIFIC TO GALATIANS?

I WANT TO
UNDERSTAND WHAT
IT MEANS TO BE
FREE IN
CHRIST

-I WANT TO STUDY
THE BIBLE
BECAUSE I WANT
IT TO BE THE
ABSOLUTE STANDARD
BY WHICH I LIVE.

I THINK IT IS
ABSOLUTELY
IMPORTANT TO
KNOW WHAT
THE BIBLE
SAYS ESP.
IN PERCEIVED
GREY AREAS

-SECONDLY, I
CONSIDER MYSELF
A BIT OF
A HISTORY BUFF/
ENTHUSIAST

Warm-up. The beginning of a new study is a good time to lay a foundation for honest sharing of ideas, to get comfortable with each other, and to encourage a sense of common purpose. Group discussion can be either stimulating or intimidating, depending on how safe people feel. Especially when you are studying a book full of truth-versus-error issues, you need to cultivate respect and acceptance so that people will be open to facing wrong thoughts and behavior. Establish the ground rules that the standard of right or wrong will be the Bible, and that no person will be rejected or carelessly hurt even when someone disagrees with someone else's views.

One way to foster common ground is to talk about what each group member hopes to get out of your group—out of your study of Galatians, and out of any prayer, singing, sharing, outreach, or anything else you might do together. Why do you want to study the Bible, and Galatians in particular? If you have someone write down each member's hopes and expectations, then you can look back at these goals later to see if they are being met. Allow about fifteen minutes for this discussion so that it does not degenerate into vague chatting.

How to use this study. If the group has never used a LifeChange study guide before, you might take a whole meeting to get acquainted, discuss your goals, and go over the "How to Use This Study" section. Then you can take a second meeting to discuss the overview. This will ensure that everyone understands the study and will give you more time to read all of Galatians and answer the overview questions.

Go over the parts of the "How to Use This Study" section that you think the group should especially notice. For example, point out the optional questions. These are available as group discussion questions, ideas for application, and suggestions for further study. It is unlikely that anyone will have time or desire to answer all the optional questions. A person might do one "Optional Application" for any given lesson. You might choose one or two "For Thought and Discussion" questions for your group discussion, or you might spend all your time on the numbered questions. If someone wants to write answers to the optional questions, suggest that he or she use a separate notebook. A notebook will also be helpful for discussion notes, prayer requests, answers to prayers, application plans, and so on.

Invite everyone to ask questions about how to use the study guide and how your discussions will go.

Reading. It is often helpful to refresh everyone's memory by reading the passage aloud before discussing the questions. Reading all of Galatians is probably unreasonable, so just read 1:1-9. Try to make the letter sound like a living person talking.

First impressions. Try to get through questions 1–5 fairly quickly. They are background to the meat of question 6. The better your statement of the overall purpose of Galatians is, the better is your foundation for studying the details. However, don't belabor this point; you'll come back to it in the review.

You might want to compare your broad outlines of Galatians to some in Bible handbooks or study Bibles. There is also a chart of Galatians.

Questions. Give everyone a chance to share questions about the historical background and the letter. It is good to clear up any confusion as early as possible. However, don't answer any questions that deal with specific passages. Write those down and let the group answer them when you get to the passages.

Greetings and **A different gospel.** Questions 9 and 10 are some interpretation questions based on 1:1-9. Encourage several group members to offer answers.

Application. Invite everyone to share answers to question 11. If application is new to some group members, you might make up some sample applications together. Choose a paragraph or verse from 1:1-9 and think of how it is relevant to you and some specific things you could each do about it.

One application that is immediately relevant is handling the conflict that inevitably arises when people seek truth. What kinds of conflict do you observe in 1:7; 2:12; and 5:17? You'll be studying these passages in more detail later, but what principles for handling this kind of conflict (in your group, for instance) can you see? Take a look at 2:9,11; 5:15,26; 6:1-5.

Wrap-up. The group leader should have read lesson two and its "For the group" section. At this point, he or she might give a short summary of what members can expect in that lesson and the coming meeting. This is a chance to whet everyone's appetite, assign any optional questions, omit any numbered questions, or forewarn members of possible difficulties.

Encourage any members who found the overview especially difficult. Some people are better at seeing the big picture than others. Some are best at analyzing a particular verse or paragraph, while others are strongest at seeing how a passage applies to their lives. Urge members to give thanks for their own and others' strengths, and to give and request help when needed. The group is a place to learn from each other. Later lessons will draw on the gifts of close analyzers as well as overviewers and appliers, practical as well as theoretical thinkers.

Prayer. Many groups like to end with singing and/or prayer. This can include songs and prayers that respond to what you've learned in Galatians or prayers for specific needs of group members. Even if your focus is on Bible study, an atmosphere of caring and praying for each other is essential to openness. Encourage members to become friends, not just fellow students.

Some people are shy about sharing personal needs or praying aloud in groups, especially before they know the other people well. If this is true of your group, then a song and/or some silent prayer, and a short closing prayer spoken by the leader, might be an appropriate end. You could also share requests and pray in pairs.

1. John R. W. Stott, *The Message of Galatians: Only One Way* (Downers Grove, IL: InterVarsity, 1968), 16.
2. Walter A. Elwell, ed., *Evangelical Dictionary of Theology* (Grand Rapids, MI: Baker, 1984), 472.

GALATIANS 1:10-24
The Source of Truth

Paul has strongly rebuked the Galatian believers for being led astray by false teachers. He has warned them that any message different from what he originally told them is error (1:6-9). Now read 1:10-24, asking God to impress on you the truth of what Paul is saying.

1. What is the main point that Paul is making in this section?

> PAUL IS SAYING THAT HIS
> AUTHORITY, HIS APOSTLESHIP
> IS FROM GOD AND NOT MAN.
>
> — IN PARTICULAR, LOOK @
> v. 12

2. Why would this be important for the Galatians to understand?

> - BECAUSE PAUL DOESN'T HAVE
> THE SAME SORY OF AUTHORITY
> THAT OTHER APOSTLES HAVE.
> - NOT AS TRADITIONAL OR ORIGINAL
> - GALATIANS NEED TO UNDERSTAND
> WHY HE IS AN AUTHORITY
> AND NOT ~~B/////~~ THE JUDAIZERS

25

> ↳ FROM DR. SCHOLER

Why is it often tempting to try to please people? Why does this seem so important?

Optional Application:
a. Have you ever changed what you intended to say because people might disagree or be upset? If so, why did people have so much power over you?
b. Is it always wrong to shape what you say according to your audience's feelings? Why or why not?
c. Today or this week, how can you avoid displeasing God by trying to please people? Think about some of the activities you will face.

God or men? (1:10-12)

3. What might Paul have done differently if he was seeking to gain approval from people? (Consider 1:6-9,11-24.)

_____

_____

_____

_____

_____

4. a. Describe one example from your current life where pleasing people and serving Christ are in conflict.

_____

_____

_____

_____

_____

b. Why does pleasing people make it impossible to be a servant of Christ (see 1:10)?

BECAUSE THE NATURE OF

MEN IS FUNDAMENTALLY

AGAINST GOD

_____

_____

Study Skill — Compare and Contrast
The ability to identify similarities and differences is invaluable for understanding nearly anything. For instance a trained eye can evaluate an unknown bush by comparing and contrasting its leaves, stalks, and seeds with those

(continued on page 27)

(continued from page 26)
of a known plant. With Scripture, we can compare a verse or paragraph to another passage. We can look at the subject, mood, choice of words, and author's intent. We can ask, "What is in this verse that is not present in the rest of the paragraph or in a similar verse nearby?" Or, "What is the common thread between these two Scriptures?" Questions like these bring details to light and reveal how the author develops his thought.

For Further Study:
Discover more of what it means to please God rather than men in John 12:42-43, Colossians 3:23-24, 1 Thessalonians 2:4-6, and 1 Peter 3:3-4.

5. a. Examine 1:11-12. How do Paul's thoughts here differ from those in 1:10?

_____

_____

_____

_____

_____

_____

b. What is similar between 1:10 and 1:11-12?

FOCUS IS ON RECEPTION OF

AUTHORITY AND GOSPEL FROM

JESUS

_____

_____

_____

Revelation (1:12). The disclosing of what was previously unknown. Here Paul speaks of truth that God communicated to him personally. Paul, in turn, communicated that truth to others (see also Ephesians 3:2-5).

specific revelation

27

6. a. How did Paul's source of truth (Galatians 1:1,12) differ from the Galatians' source of "truth" (verses 7-8)?

- THE GALATIANS' SOURCE WAS MAN.

- ~~BARNABY~~ SAYING: "DON'T GET YOUR THEOLOGY FROM A BOOK"

b. How does our source of truth differ from Paul's?

- IT IS A BOOK RATHER THAN AN APOSTLE.

- ALTHOUGH, WE ALL HAVE THE HOLY SPIRIT WORKING IN US.

Paul's authority for ministry (1:13-20)

Judaism (1:13-14). The system of beliefs and practices belonging to the Jewish people, in contrast to Christianity or Greek philosophies. Practicing Jews lived by the Old Testament according to a highly developed oral tradition (see Mark 7:6-8). In particular, the tradition explained minute applications of the first five books of the Old Testament, which were called "the Law (or Teaching) of Moses" because they contained the history and rules for living that God instructed Moses to write down. Jewish sects varied widely, but all stressed strict monotheism (belief in one God), circumcision, and rest on the Sabbath.

7. In your own words, describe Paul before God confronted him (1:13-14).

A ZEALOT OF THE FIRST ORDER.

MERCILESS

For Further Study:
For additional background on Paul's life before conversion, see Philippians 3:5-7, and Acts 8:1-3, 9:1-2, and 26:4-5.

Study Skill — Parallel Passages

Many Bibles indicate parallel passages — other Scriptures where the same event is recorded. For example, Matthew 28:1-10 and John 20:1-18 both record Christ's resurrection. The additional facts and different perspective of each passage offer us a more complete understanding. Sometimes the second passage includes background information the author assumed his readers would know.

Certain clues help us distinguish parallels from other cross-references. First the other Bible book usually deals with the same historical period. For instance, the narrative in Acts may explain in detail an event Paul mentions in a letter. A second indicator can be the length of the cross-reference, because an event often involves a section rather than a single verse.

---

8. a. Read the account of Paul's conversion in Acts 9:1-22. (Luke uses Paul's Hebrew name, Saul, until Acts 13:9 when Paul begins ministering to Gentiles.) What strikes you as especially significant about what Paul experienced?

Q 1:12 ↑

For Thought and Discussion: Why does Paul emphasize in this passage that his message and authority didn't come from men?

great commission! Jesus

Optional Application: What is your authority for the message you proclaim? Is it people?

relates to Q6a,b

For Thought and Discussion:

a. Do you think a Christian can be too dependent on others in his or her quest for spiritual understanding? What would be the evidence and problems of that condition?

b. On the other hand, what are the dangers of being completely independent of others for one's beliefs?

c. How can one strike a sound balance between these two errors?

→ Yes, easily lead astray by false teachings

→ HERESY

→ CHURCH w/ CAREFUL INDEPENDENT STUDY

b. What do you think went through his mind during this time of tremendous change?

_____

_____

_____

_____

_____

_____

Gentiles (1:16; 2:7). Literally, "nations" or "peoples." The Jews used this term for all non-Jews. Most Jews, especially those living in Judea under Roman oppression, regarded Gentiles with animosity and disdain (see Acts 10:28,45; Ephesians 2:11-19).

Arabia (1:17). The desert region to the east and south of Palestine. Paul is apparently referring to the area ruled by the Nabatean kingdom under King Aretas, which extended from the Sinai Peninsula to the Euphrates River.
     Paul seems to be saying that his first response was to spend time alone with God. From 4:25, some have conjectured that he traveled as far as Mount Sinai to receive his revelation from God. Although this would provide a good parallel with the ministries of Moses and Elijah, it is more probable that he stayed near Damascus because he returned there (see 1:17).
     In 2 Corinthians 11:32-33, Paul writes that Aretas tried to have Paul arrested in Damascus. Paul may have started preaching to the Gentiles while in Nabatean Arabia, thereby arousing the king's ire.

---

9. Why do you think it was so important to Paul that he not consult men?

BECAUSE IT EMPHASIZES THAT HIS APOSTOLIC AUTHORITY IS FULLY VESTED BY JESUS ALONE, JUST AS IT WAS FOR THE ORIGINAL 12

_____

_____

Paul's early ministry (1:21-24)

Find Damascus, Syria, and Cilicia on the Map of Paul's Missionary Journey. Although Paul gave the Jewish community in foreign cities the first opportunity to hear the gospel (see Acts 14:1), his primary calling was to the Gentiles (see Galatians 1:16).

10. In summary, how would you respond to the argument that the false teachers had more authority than Paul because they came from Judea, the center of Judaism and the home of the apostles?

_____

_____

_____

_____

_____

For Thought and Discussion:

a. Describe Paul's earliest witnessing in Acts 9:20-30.

b. Why would God send someone so knowledgeable and with such close ties to Judaism to Gentile lands (see also Acts 22:17-21)?

Optional Application:

Meditate on how discovering Jesus has changed your life. Thank God for that.

this 7

Your response

11. Fill in the contrasts for "Motive in Ministry" and "Source of Truth" on the Alternatives in Galatians chart on page 33.

Study Skill — Application

When looking for a truth to apply to your life, ask yourself these questions about the passage you are studying:

Is there a *sin* here for me to confess or avoid? (Do I need to make restitution or ask someone's forgiveness?)

Is there a *promise* to claim and live by? (Does this promise apply to me, or just to the original readers? Have I met the conditions for claiming this promise?)

(continued on page 32)

(continued from page 31)

For Thought and Discussion: Do you think that those who do not have a dramatic change in their lives at conversion are at a disadvantage in testifying about Jesus or in growing more holy? Why or why not?

Do I need to change an *attitude*? (How can I go about this?)

Is there a *command* to obey? (Am I willing to do this no matter how I feel?)

Is there an *example* to follow or avoid?

Is there something to *pray* or *praise* God about?

What difference does this *truth* about the Father, Jesus Christ, or the Holy Spirit make to me?

12. Review 1:10-24 and the answers you've written, and look at the marginal questions in this lesson. What one insight leaps out as something you would like to apply to your own life?

V. 10

-THAT, MUCH IN MANY WAYS, I ACT TO PLEASE men AND not GOD

- I SERVE TO HELP BUT THERE IS AN UNDERLYING MOTIVATION FOR OTHERS TO APPROVE OF ME.

13. How would you like this truth to affect the way you think and act?

14. What one step can you take this week to begin cooperating with God in making this happen? How can you act on this truth?

32

Alternatives in Galatians

ISSUE/PASSAGE	WAY OF TRUTH	WAY OF ERROR
Message to Follow (1:6-7)	*gospel of Christ*	*different "gospel"*
Motive in Ministry (1:10)	approval of God	approval of MEN
Source of Truth (1:11-12)	JESUS CHRIST	MAN
Circle of Fellowship (2:11-14)		
Standing Before God (2:16)		
Gift of the Spirit (3:2,5)		
Christian Maturity (3:3)		
Inheritance from Father (3:18)		
Relationship to God (4:6-7)		
Jewish Customs & Law (4:31; 5:1)		
Use of Freedom (5:13)		
Direction for Life (5:16-17)		
Consequences of Actions (6:8-9)		
What Really Matters (6:12,15)		

(handwritten margin notes, left side:) HOW DID GOD CHANGE OUR LIVES? LIKE PAUL? IF TIMID END

(handwritten margin notes, lower left:) FOR PEOPLE LEADING, THERE IS A GUIDE @ THE END OF A CHAPTER

15. Write down any questions you have about 1:10-24.

_____

_____

_____

_____

_____

For the group

Warm-up. People usually come to Bible study full of the day's busyness. It takes a little time to change gears to being internally quiet and open with other believers. Beginning with worship and prayer helps people shift mental gears. Another aid is to begin with a question related to the passage at hand that draws on people's personal feelings and experiences. For this lesson, try asking each group member to tell one way in which knowing God has changed his or her life. This will help everyone identify with Paul and get to know each other at the same time.

Read aloud. Ask someone to read 1:10-24 aloud as though it were Paul speaking. Try to express the mood of the passage when you read.

Summarize. Questions 1 and 2 are meant to give you a look at the forest before you examine the trees in detail. Have one or two people tell what 1:10-24 is basically about. If the answers are not perfect now, don't belabor the issue; you can come back to a fuller summary at the end of your discussion.

Questions. Focusing on one or two specific areas can be more helpful than trying to look at everything in a passage. People will remember one or two key points and understand a few steps they can take for growth. Prayerfully choose which topic(s) would be most vital for your group. In addition to the numbered and optional questions, consider the following:

1. Today we have the opportunity to recognize Paul's authority in our response to about 30 percent

of the New Testament Scriptures. What difference will it make in your approach if you view Galatians and Paul's other letters as the Word of God rather than the word of man?

2. Francis Schaeffer compared one's view of Scripture to a continental divide or "watershed." Two neighboring flakes of snow may end up thousands of miles apart during the spring run-off. "It is obeying the Scriptures which really is the watershed. We can say the Bible is without mistake and still destroy it if we bend the Scriptures by our lives to fit this culture instead of judging the culture by Scripture."[1] How is this remark relevant to the Galatian situation? To believers in our nation? How have the traditions of men replaced the ways of God? In what areas do you find it easy to ignore or rationalize God's truth? — *STREAM/DL MUSIC*

ALTHOUGH IT WAS NOT SCRIPTURE YET?

JUDAIZERS BENDING SCRIPTURE TO JEWISH CULTURE

3. The Judaizers wanted Gentile believers to become Jews in order to please non-Christian Jews. Paul insisted on freedom not because he wanted to please the Gentiles but because he wanted to please God. Examine some of your practices. Do you do any of them to please other people rather than God?

↳ *LEADING THIS SUNDAY SCHOOL?*

1. Francis Schaeffer, *The Great Evangelical Disaster* (Westchester, IL: Crossway, 1984), 63.

GO OVER HW

PREFACE:

SAY "MY FOCUS IS ON THE AUTHORITY OF SCRIPTURE"

READ PASSAGE

Q1, Q2

PG 30 OPT APP

PG 30 FOR THOUGHT & DISC

Q 11

PG 35 Q2

RESPONSE, IF NO TIME HIGHLY ENCOURAGE

GALATIANS 2:1-10

Confirmation of the Truth

Paul has admonished the Galatians for turning away from the truth of the gospel. The truth they originally embraced, and then rejected, came from his lips! So Paul pointed out in chapter 1 that he got this truth from God Himself, not from human authorities.

To underscore the authority of his message, Paul describes his contacts with those in the early church recognized as its human authorities. Read 2:1-10 a couple of times, asking yourself, "How does this information contribute to the point Paul wants to make?"

1 What prompted Paul's trip to Jerusalem?

A revelation from God

2. Briefly describe the individuals involved in this incident.

Barnabas (see Acts 4:36-37; 11:22-26)

Optional Application: What traits do you find in Barnabas, Peter, or another character that are worthy of your imitation? How can you put one of those traits into practice?

_____

_____

_____

Peter (see Acts 4:13; Galatians 2:7-9)

_____

_____

_____

_____

John (see Acts 4:13; Galatians 2:9)

_____

_____

_____

_____

Titus (see 2 Corinthians 8:23; Galatians 2:3)

_____

_____

_____

_____

James (see Galatians 1:19; 2:9)

_____

_____

_____

_____

For Further Study: Do a character study on Barnabas (see Acts 4:32-37; 9:26-27; 11:22-26; 13:1-15:39).

For Thought and Discussion: In chapter 1, Paul affirmed that his message came clearly from God. Why, fourteen years later, would he fear that he had been wrong (see 2:2)?

The conflict (2:1-5)

3. Why do you think Paul met privately with the leaders rather than seeking a public forum?

_____

_____

_____

_____

_____

_____

Circumcision (2:3). A cutting away of the foreskin. Every Jewish male and every foreign male who became part of the nation was circumcised as a sign of God's covenant with Israel (see Genesis 17:10-14; Leviticus 12:3). The rite signified

For Thought and Discussion: Consider how Paul handled the strife in 2:1-5. What aspects of this are worthy of imitation?

Optional Application: When it came to issues of truth, Paul would not give in. Do you ever allow error to stand unchallenged? If so, prayerfully consider how cutting remarks, irreverent jests, fatalistic discouragement, wrong values, or unethical behavior should be resisted. Determine to speak the truth in love (see Proverbs 25:26; Ephesians 4:15), and ask God for specific guidance on how to do it in your situation.

an invitation for God to cut the man off from his life and his people if he ever broke the covenant.

4. The issue of this visit to Jerusalem — perhaps the same event[1] — is the focus of Paul's visit to Jerusalem in Acts 15. Read at least Acts 15:1-11. What does this add to your understanding of the conflict?

_____

_____

_____

_____

_____

Freedom (2:4). *Free* and *freedom* occur eleven times in Galatians. *Free* means "not under the control or power of another."[2]

Freedom ***in Christ Jesus***, is the believer's liberty or release from all that restrains unhindered devotion to God. It is not just an ability to make choices; it is the ability to make right choices for truth, love, purity, and fullness of life. It is never independence from God, but obedience to the true God (see Romans 6:16-23). The concept of man autonomous from God not only violates the reality of the universe we live in, it also diminishes human capability and fulfillment for both this life and eternity.

The believer's freedom comes through his death with Christ (see Romans 7:1-6) and is expressed in the new life given by God's indwelling Spirit (see 2 Corinthians 3:6,17).

5. What does the Bible say the Christian is free from in the following verses?

John 8:31-36; Romans 6:6-7 _____

_____

Romans 8:2-3; Galatians 3:23-25 _____

_____

Galatians 4:8 _____

_____

Hebrews 2:14-15 _____

_____

_____

False believers (2:4). Why did these Jewish Christians insist that to be part of God's people one had to live like a Jew? Possibly because they feared persecution from zealous Jews or rejection from their kinsmen if they agreed that the covenant of Moses was superceded (see 6:12). Possibly they also couldn't imagine that God would change His covenant. They had been raised to feel that circumcision, the dietary laws, and the rest were all essential to being right with God, and they hadn't grasped the implications of the Cross and the new covenant Jesus proclaimed (see Luke 22:20).

6. On what basis do you think Paul identified these supposed brothers as "false"?

_____

_____

_____

_____

_____

7. a. What was his response to their strategy?

_____

_____

_____

_____

Optional Application: Are you wise and loving when you confront error, or do you seem judgmental and effect little benefit? How can you grow in this area?

For Thought and Discussion:
a. Are people today ever pressured to conform to an "acceptable" lifestyle in order to be Christian? If so, how have you observed this?

b. Do you think Paul would find modern Christian rules more justifiable than the Jewish ones he opposed? Why or why not?

c. What are the implications of these conclusions for your life?

Optional Application: Do you ever act as though God judges by external appearance (see 2:6)? If so, how? What do you need to change?

For Thought and Discussion: Suppose God called you to share the gospel with people of a different culture. How would you decide which American Christian practices could be abandoned and which could not?

b. What does this response tell you about Paul's values?

_____

_____

_____

_____

The resolution (2:6-10)

8. Do you think Paul was disrespectful of the church leaders? Explain.

_____

_____

_____

_____

9. What do you learn from Paul's perspective on position and status in the church (see 2:6)?

_____

_____

_____

_____

10. Why was it important to Paul that the leaders of the Jerusalem church added nothing to his message?

_____

_____

_____

_____

11. In order for Paul to minister in harmony with the other apostles, he had to arrive at certain understandings with them. What did they have in common, and how did they agree to be different?

commonalities	differences

12. What does it mean to see God at work in someone's ministry (see 2:8)?

_____

_____

_____

_____

_____

The grace given to me (2:9). Grace is the undeserved favor God shows to man. Although we quickly think of being saved by grace (see Ephesians 2:8), grace is also given for fruitful service (see Romans 12:6).

Optional Application: If you know of any believers who are struggling financially, do something that will help and encourage them as a sign of your oneness in Christ (see 2:10).

Fellowship (2:9). Partnership in God's work and sharing in the same life that comes from Christ.

Poor (2:10). The poor believers in Jerusalem (see Acts 11:28-29). Famine and persecution seem to have impoverished the Jerusalem church.

13. How would Paul's remembering the poor Jewish believers in Jerusalem be significant in the Jewish-Gentile conflict (see also Romans 15:25-27)?

_____

_____

_____

_____

_____

Your response

14. What impact do you think the decisions of 2:1-10 probably had on the early church?

_____

_____

_____

_____

15. How are these issues relevant to your life? (Write down at least one implication that you want to focus on for further growth.)

_____

_____

_____

_____

44

16. What action would you like to take in light of this relevance?

_____

_____

_____

_____

_____

17. List any questions you have about 2:1-10.

_____

_____

_____

_____

_____

For the group

Warm-up. Ask everyone to recall a conflict in a church he or she has been a part of. You don't need to mention the various situations. Just let the memories set a context for discussing 2:1-10.

Read aloud and summarize 2:1-10.

Questions. The following are some possible ways of focusing your discussion. You probably can't cover all of them, so choose what you think will help your group most.
    The first level of 2:1-10 is the original disagreement Paul faced. Explore what the conflict was, how it was resolved, and why it is important to us. What would your lives be like if the church had decided that it really was necessary for Christians to live like Jews?
    The next level is examining 2:1-10 as a model for resolving conflict. When a question or disagreement arises, it is often easier to remain silent than to bring it up before others. Talk about the benefits of open discussion of disagreements. Also discuss

45

some of the fears and dangers: What if I'm wrong? What if someone else is a better debater than I, and I don't know how to resist him? What if we can't come to agreement? What if he or she doesn't like me anymore?

This passage might give one the impression that Paul felt he was above criticism—perhaps even close-minded and unwilling to change. Philippians 3:12-14 gives a different picture. Use this as a basis to discuss in what areas of the Christian life we should be unyielding, and in what areas we should be humble and pliable. Also consider when you should make an issue of something and when you should overlook it.

Summarize and wrap-up.

Prayer. Take to God any conflicts you are currently facing with anyone. Ask for the wisdom to deal with them in the most godly manner. Praise God for sending an apostle to Gentiles and for safeguarding your freedom in Christ Jesus. Ask Him to show you how to live in freedom this week.

1. Opinions vary as to how Acts 15:1-29 and Galatians 2:1-10 are related. Some people think they describe the same occasion, and some don't. For a fair treatment of the various possibilities, see Donald Guthrie, *Galatians* (Grand Rapids, MI: Eerdmans, 1973), 29–36.
2. David B. Guralnik, ed., *Webster's New World Dictionary of the American Language*, pocket-sized ed. (New York: World Publishing, 1959), 219.

GALATIANS 2:11-21

Contending for the Truth

We've seen that Paul sought to make sure that his own life and ministry, as well as those of others, were based on God's truth rather than man's ideas.

1. Recall Paul's previous contacts with Peter (1:18; 2:7-9). How would you describe their earlier relationship and regard for one another?

_____

_____

_____

_____

_____

Study Skill—
Rereading with Varied Perspectives
Repeated observation is one of the most fundamental steps in learning. By changing one's perspective or by approaching with different questions, fresh insights are gained. A valuable habit is to read a passage once for an overview, followed by a second reading for detailed analysis. Another recommended practice is to ask new questions with each additional reading, such as "What people are involved in this drama?" or "What wrong ideas was Paul trying to change?"

For Further Study:
Compare what Peter
learned in Caesarea
and Joppa (see Acts
10:1–11:18) to his later
behavior in Antioch
(see Galatians 2:11-16).
Have you ever been
like this?

**Optional
Application:**
Peter believed and
preached a gospel
of faith, yet in this
instance his life
contradicted his
message. Does your
life reflect a gospel
of rules or of grace?
What do you think
you need to change?

2. Now read 2:11-21. In what way does this passage
continue the case that Paul has been building
so far in this letter?

_____

_____

_____

_____

_____

Antioch (2:11). Antioch in Syria was the third larg-
est city in the Roman Empire. Because it was
so close to the eastern edge of the Empire, its
population of 500,000 represented a wide mix
of nationalities and religious pursuits. It was a
wealthy commercial center with a correspond-
ing emphasis on luxury and sensuality.

Antioch was one of the first places where
the gospel was preached to Gentiles. The
response was so great that the apostles sent
Barnabas to help, and Barnabas soon invited
Paul to join him. The Church established there
became the home base for Paul's missionary
travels (see Acts 11:19-26; 13:1-3).

The conflict (2:11-14)

3. What did Peter do in Antioch that made Paul
angry (2:11-12)?

_____

_____

_____

_____

4. Why did Peter do this?

_____

48

_____

_____

_____

For Thought and Discussion: Can you think of church behavior today that deserves to be called "hypocrisy" (see 2:13)? Explain.

Eating with Gentiles (2:12). This was taboo for strict Jews. One might eat food "unclean" according to the Old Testament dietary laws (see Leviticus 11) or food that had been sacrificed in idol worship, which was often sold in the public market (see 1 Corinthians 10:25-28).

Even if the food itself was pure, the Jews believed that contact by touch could make both food and person unclean. Mosaic laws designed to quarantine disease (see Numbers 19:11-22; Haggai 2:12-13) were applied to externally separate Jews from paganism. Close association with Gentiles would physically link a Jew to all kinds of evil practices. In addition, many devout Jews followed such detailed rules of seating, blessings, serving, and etiquette that eating with Gentiles was difficult, if not impossible.[1]

Jesus Christ rejected this emphasis on external defilement during His earthly life (see Mark 7:14-19; Luke 5:30-31). In His death, Christ removed the legal (including dietary) barrier to fellowship (see Ephesians 2:14-16).

For Further Study:
a. Peter himself was probably the first to preach the gospel to Gentiles. In Acts 10:27-29,48 and 11:2, identify ways in which Peter had been living "like a Gentile" (Galatians 2:14).

b. Read Peter's later reference to this ministry to the Gentiles in Acts 15:5-11. Why would he have acknowledged that it was wrong to "force Gentiles to follow Jewish customs" (Galatians 2:14)?

Circumcision group (2:12). Those among the Jewish Christians who believed Gentiles needed to be circumcised in order to be part of the church (see Acts 15:5). Some of this group, perhaps on business from James, were visiting Antioch from Jerusalem. Perhaps Peter feared that the report they might carry back home would undermine his reputation, hinder evangelism among Jews, or even lead to attack from Gentile-hating militants who wanted to drive all Gentiles (especially Romans) from Jewish soil.[2]

5. Why did Paul call the behavior of the Jewish believers who withdrew from the Gentiles "hypocrisy" (2:13; see 2:14-16)?

_____

For Thought and Discussion: Imagine you are visiting a church that some members of your own church disapprove of but that you think is valid. Now imagine that the disapprovers walk in. What will you do? Sneak out? Pretend you are not participating?

For Thought and Discussion: Do you think Paul was right to rebuke Peter publicly? Form some guidelines about when public confrontation is right or wrong (see Matthew 18:15-17; 1 Corinthians 6:1-8; Ephesians 5:11; 1 Timothy 5:1,19-20; Titus 1:9-16).

_____

_____

_____

_____

_____

6. List Paul's reasons for publicly confronting his brothers (2:11-14).

_____

_____

_____

_____

_____

The argument (2:15-21)

Paul now gives the reasoning behind his intervention.

Justified (2:16-17). God's pronouncement, as Judge, that a person is free from punishment due for his wrong-doing, declared "not guilty," restored to favor and covenant relationship with God, and given all the privileges of one who has perfectly kept the Law. God is just in doing this because Christ satisfied all God's legal demands for Himself and anyone who belongs to Him (see Romans 3:25-26).

Among the Jews, justification meant God's declaration that a person or group really was part of His covenant people and in right relationship to Him. The requirement for belonging to the covenant people had always been circumcision and obedience to the Law. Now, however, the requirement is being united with Christ. Jesus is the Father's obedient subject, so His obedient subjects and friends are the Father's, too.

7. Describe what justification accomplishes, according to the following verses. First write what the verse *says* (observation), then what this *means* in your own words (interpretation).

Romans 5:1_____

_____

_____

meaning _____

_____

_____

Romans 5:18_____

_____

_____

meaning _____

_____

_____

Romans 8:33-34_____

_____

_____

meaning _____

_____

_____

Law (2:16). A system of rules established by authority or custom. Here, and throughout most of Galatians, this term refers to the Law of Moses. Its commandments are found in the Old Testament books of Genesis through Deuteronomy. The Law encompassed all areas of life from religious sacrifice to moral behavior to economic and agricultural regulations. Many Jews felt that as they carefully observed

Optional Application: What practical difference does it make that you have been crucified with Christ (see 2:20)? How can you "live by faith in the Son of God" this week?

these instructions, God would be obliged to recognize their good deeds. Others believed that they were part of God's people by grace, but that keeping all these rules was a necessary response to God's grace.

In other places in Galatians, Paul uses the term "law" of law in general (5:23), of the Old Testament books that contain the Law (4:21), and of the "law of Christ" (6:2).

8. Why can't the Law justify us (see Romans 3:10-20; Galatians 2:15-16)?

_____

_____

_____

_____

_____

9. What do you learn about the meaning of faith from the following Scriptures?

Romans 4:18-21 _____

_____

_____

Hebrews 11:1-2,6 _____

_____

_____

10. What are we supposed to have faith about?

John 14:1_____

_____

_____

_____

52

Acts 2:36 _____

_____

_____

_____

Romans 10:9-13 _____

_____

_____

_____

1 Corinthians 15:1-7,14,17 _____

_____

_____

_____

11. Faith can mean both faith in a person and faith
in a piece of truth. Based on your answers to
questions 9 and 10, define faith in Christ without using the word *believe*. (In Greek, *faith* is
simply the noun form of the verb *to believe*.)

_____

_____

_____

_____

_____

12. Explain the following statements in your own
words.

Paul's relationship to the Law: "through the law
I died to the law" (2:19).

_____

_____

_____

For Further Study:
How does Christ's
death make a believer
dead to the Law?
What are some other
implications of your
death with Christ (see
Romans 6:1-14; 7:1-6;
2 Corinthians 5:14-15;
Colossians 3:1-5)?

**For Thought and
Discussion:**
a. What is the
practical, day-to-day
significance of your
crucifixion with
Christ?
b. How does hav-
ing Christ's life within
you affect you in
practical ways?

**For Thought and
Discussion:** Explain
2:17-18 in your own
words.

_____

_____

_____

Paul's relationship to Christ: "I have been crucified with Christ and I no longer live, but Christ
lives in me" (2:20).

_____

_____

_____

_____

_____

_____

_____

13. What key aspects of the gospel were threatened
by a pursuit of righteousness through law (see
2:21)?

_____

_____

_____

_____

14. If obeying rules isn't what makes God accept
us, what keeps us from sinning flagrantly? How
does our dying and new life (see 2:17-20) pre-
vent this?

_____

_____

_____

_____

54

Your response

15. Summarize why Christians are not obliged to keep the Jewish law (see 2:15-21).

    2:16 _____

    _____

    _____

    2:19 _____

    _____

    _____

    2:21 _____

    _____

    _____

16. Fill in answers for "Circle of Fellowship" and "Standing Before God" on the Alternatives in Galatians chart on page 33.

17. What one insight from 2:11-21 stands out as something you want to apply to your life?

    _____

    _____

    _____

    _____

    _____

18. How would you like this truth to affect your life?

    _____

    _____

    _____

    _____

    _____

For Further Study: Read Jesus' and Paul's attitudes toward the moral laws of the Old Testament (see Matthew 22:34-40; Romans 13:8-10; Galatians 5:13-14). Are we free from having to keep these commands? Do we earn God's acceptance by keeping them?

Optional Application: Who looks to you for standards of behavior, as some men looked to Peter? What can you do to see that your behavior communicates faith in a God who saves and helps sinners, rather than faith in your ability to perform?

19. What one step can you take this week to put this into practice?

_____

_____

_____

_____

_____

20. List any questions you have about 2:11-21.

_____

_____

_____

_____

_____

For the group

Warm-up. Ask, "Have you ever been pressured by another Christian to conform to a set of rules?" Give everyone a chance to describe his or her experiences briefly.

Read aloud and summarize.

Questions. Here are some possible topics of discussion:

We often avoid confronting people about error and let them continue in their misconceptions. Have group members identify situations where they should challenge inappropriate behavior. Look for the best way to go about it.

The pressure to conform to the practice of those around us is strong. Ask the group whether fear of people or the desire to fit in has recently tempted them to act contrary to God's truth. How can you avoid giving in to this temptation?

It is possible that some in the group are trying to please God by doing good, but aren't even His children yet. Ask, "Do you think a person can depend on rules and still have faith in Christ?" or "Paul indicates that there are people who aren't accepted by God because they seek His approval in the wrong way. How do you know you aren't one?"

Be sensitive. Distinguish what opens doors for discussion and learn from what is too threatening and produces resistance.

Summarize and wrap-up.

Prayer. Thank God that you are acceptable to God just because you have put your faith in Christ, not because of any rules you keep. Ask God to show you how to live by faith in His Son, to live as those who have been crucified with Christ.

1. William Hendriksen, *Exposition of Galatians* (Grand Rapids, MI: Baker, 1968), 92. See also Alfred Edersheim, *The Life and Times of Jesus the Messiah*, one-volume ed. (Grand Rapids, MI: Eerdmans, 1971), 206–210.
2. F. F. Bruce, *The Epistle to the Galatians* (Grand Rapids, MI: Eerdmans, 1982), 130.

GALATIANS 3:1-14

Living by Faith

So far, Paul has been defending his authority
and the gospel as he originally taught it to the
Galatians.

1. Read 3:1-14. How does this passage differ from
   the earlier chapters of Galatians?

   _____

   _____

   _____

   _____

   _____

   _____

   _____

2. List all the contrasts and opposites Paul uses in
   this passage.

   _____

   _____

   _____

   _____

   _____

   _____

   _____

For Thought and Discussion: Could a person do the same activity with human effort as he could with the Spirit's power? If not, why not? If so, what would be the difference?

3. Of the contrasts on page 59, which do you think best portrays the message of 3:1-14?

_____

_____

Study Skill — Outlining

Outlining is an excellent way to picture what an author is saying. First, summarize the main point of each section or paragraph in a short, clear statement. Ask, "What common thread runs through each sentence or thought in this section?" Often a word or phrase from the passage itself will be the clue, although you may want to force yourself to think through the meaning by using your own words.

Next look for the subdivisions of that thought. Ask, "How does this sentence or thought relate to the main paragraph? Which sentences fit together?" and "Where does a new thought begin?" You will sometimes need to discover the subpoints first in order to fit them into a single main point.

The points on the same level of an outline should parallel one another. For example, if (1) is a command, then (2) should be a command.

---

4. As you reread 3:1-14, make your own outline. The first section is done as an example. If you wish, re-do it or subdivide the subpoints to further examine the passage.

(3:1-5)   Continue the same way you started.

(3:1-2)   Did you start with faith in Christ or human effort?

(3:3-4)   Will you finish by faith or human effort?

(3:5)   Is your present spiritual experience based on faith or human effort?

(3:6-9) _____

_____

_____

_____

_____

_____

(3:10-14) _____

_____

_____

_____

_____

_____

A good beginning (3:1-5)

Foolish (3:1). "[A]n attitude of *heart* as well as a quality of *mind*. It refers not to bluntness but to a sinful neglect to use one's mental power to the best advantage . . . not necessarily dull, but thoughtless . . . not stupid, but foolish."[1]

---

5. Why is it "foolish" and "bewitched" (3:1) to choose human effort over the Spirit? Find all the reasons you can in 3:1-5, and add any others you can think of.

_____

_____

_____

_____

_____

_____

_____

For Thought and Discussion: What logical connections can you see between 3:1 and the preceding verses (see 2:20-21)?

For Thought and Discussion: The Galatians were not in Jerusalem when Jesus was crucified, so what does Paul mean by saying, "Before your very eyes Jesus Christ was clearly portrayed as crucified" (3:1)?

Optional Application: Are you living daily on the same basis by which you were saved? How can you live by the Spirit this week?

For Further Study:
Read Luke 5:1-11.
Have you had similar
experiences of fruit-
less human effort or
of great reward for
trust in Christ?

**Optional
Application:** Paul
says believing what
you hear is the key to
seeing God's power
(see 3:5). As you read
your Bible this week,
write down not what
it says you should do,
but what it says God
will do. Thank Him,
and be ready (in the
right place, attitude,
activity) to see Him
work.

For Further Study:
Why did promise and
faith take precedence
over physical ancestry
in deciding who were
"Abraham's children"
(see Genesis 21:8-12
and Romans 9:6-8)?

Trying to finish by means of the flesh (3:3).
To finish, complete, or bring to an end.[2]
The identical contrast of words—begin and
complete—is in Philippians 1:6, where God
continues to work His maturing process until
the day Christ returns.

Have you experienced so much . . . in vain? (3:4).
Like Paul, the Galatian believers had probably
been persecuted by both unbelieving Jews and
Gentiles (see Acts 14:19–15:22). If they rejected
the truth they originally stood for, their suffering would have served no purpose. Besides, this
persecution had been stirred up by Jews! If they
wanted to act just like another variation of Judaism, this would be acceptable to the Jews and
legally recognized by the civil authorities. Paul
expresses hope that this is not really true.

Consider Abraham (3:6-9)

Abraham (3:6). Genesis 15:1-6 tells the events
behind Galatians 3:6. Abraham was in his late
seventies or early eighties when God promised
him a son. His wife, Sarah, was around seventy
and had never had a child. Consider the obsta-
cles Abraham faced in believing what God said.

Blessed (3:8-9). A blessed person is the object of divine
favor, resulting in spiritual and often material
well-being, prosperity, and success (see Genesis
24:1,34-35; Ephesians 1:3). As with the contrasting curse (see Galatians 3:10-14), it is based on the
word that God has given. To bless means to speak
well of someone. God's well-speaking is a promise
that will be fulfilled (see 3:14).

6. According to Genesis 15:6 and Galatians 3:6,
   on what basis did God reckon Abraham as righteous (in right standing) before Him?

   _____

   _____

   _____

7. The Jews claimed to be the children of Abraham—that is, the heirs of God's promises to him. From your answer to question 6, whom would you conclude should be the true children of Abraham? (Compare Galatians 3:7.)

_____

_____

_____

_____

8. Think about the kind of faith Abraham had to have to believe God would give him a son at the age of eighty. What does this tell you about the kind of faith in Christ that a person needs to have?

_____

_____

_____

_____

Redeemed from a curse (3:10-14)

9. Why wouldn't a person be blessed if he or she kept most of the Law (3:10)?

_____

_____

_____

_____

10. What do you think 3:10-12 is saying you would experience if you tried to win God's blessing by rules and self-effort?

_____

_____

_____

Optional Application: Pause right now and thank God that you already have His blessing. Meditate on what that means for your life.

For Thought and Discussion: The Jews thought the promised blessings were only for Abraham's biological descendants. However, what God really said was that all nations would be blessed through Abraham (see Genesis 12:1-3; Galatians 3:8-9). Why is it important to you that God promised all along to bless you?

For Thought and Discussion: How could it be fair for God to expect anyone to keep the whole Law?

63

_____

_____

_____

Redeem (3:13). To deliver from bondage by paying a price. This word was used of purchasing one who had been enslaved in order to free him.[3]

---

11. What happened to the curse that went along with violation of the Law (3:13-14)?

_____

_____

_____

_____

Your response

12. In question 5 you wrote some reasons why you would be foolish to try to grow and minister by human effort. To summarize 3:1-14, state the three main reasons Paul gives for living by the Spirit and faith rather than by self-effort.

3:1-5 _____

_____

3:6-9 _____

_____

3:10-14 _____

_____

13. Fill in "Gift of the Spirit" and "Christian Maturity" on the Alternatives in Galatians chart on page 33.

14. What truth from 3:1-14 seems most personally significant to you today?

_____

_____

_____

_____

_____

15. How would you like this insight to affect your life?

_____

_____

_____

_____

_____

16. What step can you take this week to begin letting this happen?

_____

_____

_____

_____

_____

17. List any questions you have about 3:1-14.

_____

_____

_____

_____

For Thought and Discussion:
The original issue between Paul and the Judaizers was circumcision and other Jewish rules of cleanliness (see 2:3,11-13). However, in chapter 3, do you think Paul is expanding his argument to include moral laws kept by self-effort rather than by the Spirit? Why or why not?

For Thought and Discussion:
a. Why wouldn't it be better if God made us work for His blessings?
b. If God's blessings come solely by faith, where does human effort come in?

For the group

Warm-up. Ask, "When you became a Christian, did you feel that you were welcomed into the Christian community because you agreed to live by the rules or because you had accepted God's offer of forgiveness? Briefly describe why you felt that way."

Questions. We sometimes assume that everyone else thinks as we do. Or, we fear that no one else does. Encourage group members to share their own thoughts freely and to ask questions of one another.

Choose your issues according to the group's needs. It may be important to deal with the balancing issue of where works and human effort fit into the Christian life. But if your group is oriented toward duty and drudgery, it may be more important to focus only on the role of faith.

The message of this passage should revolutionize the way Christians live. The believer's daily walk is intended to be a continuation of the way he was saved (compare Colossians 2:6-7). Faith in what God has spoken brings the power of the Spirit into our lives.

Prayer. Thank God for providing the power of His Spirit to save you, to enable you to live daily, and to bring you to full maturity. Thank Him that you don't have to rely on your own strength. Thank Him for releasing you from the curse of the Law. Ask Him to make you more and more like Abraham in his faith.

1. William Hendriksen, *Exposition of Galatians* (Grand Rapids, MI: Baker, 1968), 92. See also Alfred Edersheim, *The Life and Times of Jesus the Messiah*, one-volume ed. (Grand Rapids, MI: Eerdmans, 1971), 111.
2. William F. Arndt and F. Wilbur Gingrich, *A Greek-English Lexicon of the New Testament and Other Early Christian Literature* (Chicago: University of Chicago Press, 1957), 302.
3. W. E. Vine, *An Expository Dictionary of New Testament Words*, vol. 2 (Old Tappan, NJ: Revell, 1952), 263.

GALATIANS 3:15-25

The Priority of the Promise

Paul continues to develop his case from the life of Abraham. To follow the context, read 3:6-25.

1. How would you state the position Paul is defending throughout chapter 3?

_____

_____

_____

_____

_____

For Thought and Discussion: Why should Abraham also be important for those of us who are not Jewish (see 3:7-9,14)?

Abraham was one of the most important figures in Jewish history. Rabbinic discussions of law and custom often appealed to his precedent.

An enduring promise (3:15-18)

Covenant (3:15). An agreement made between two parties. The word can mean "treaty," "pact," "contract," or "will." A marriage covenant, business contract, or political treaty is usually two-sided; each party makes certain promises to the other. God's agreement with Abraham, however, was thoroughly one-sided; He made promises, and Abraham had only to accept them. Because of this one-sidedness and because 3:18 emphasizes inheritance, *covenant*

Optional Application: How aware are you of God's promises? List as many promises as you can that God has given to His church. How do you live and think differently when, in faith, you expect Him to fulfill those promises? (Consider Matthew 6:31-33; John 15:9-17; Romans 8:28-29; Hebrews 13:4-6; 1 John 5:11-15.)

Optional Application: How secure are you in God's promises? Are there areas in you where fear is stronger than faith? Select a passage where God promises His provision in that area (see 1 Peter 1:3-4). Write it out and place it where you will see it at least once a day. Memorize it. Ask God to write it on your heart.

is often translated as "will" in 3:15,17. Yet the One who made the promises is ever-living![1]

Duly established (3:15). All proper legal formalities were completed, so no one but the testator (God) can change the will.

2. What is the point of the analogy between God's covenant and a human legal agreement (3:15-18)?

_____

_____

_____

_____

_____

3. How secure was God's covenant with Abraham? (*Optional:* See Leviticus 26:42-45; 2 Kings 13:22-23; Romans 11:25-29; Hebrews 6:13-17.)

_____

_____

_____

_____

_____

Seed (3:16). The offspring descended from an individual. The same word is used in the plant kingdom, where the seed produced represents the continuation of the kind (see Genesis 1:12; John 8:39). Although the singular word *seed* is often used in a collective sense (see Galatians 3:29), it can also refer to one specific individual among the many descendants (see Genesis 21:13; 2 Samuel 7:12).

4. What did Abraham have to do to receive the promise of relationship with God (3:6)?

_____

_____

_____

Optional Application: What would living by God's promises mean in your situation?

5. The Jews believed that the Law given to Moses added extra requirements for receiving the promise. Were they right, or was faith in God still the only requirement (see 3:15-18)?

_____

_____

_____

For Thought and Discussion: Why did God give the Law instead of sending Christ sooner? Are there any parallels with our present wait for Christ's return?

6. What difference does it make to you that your relationship with God and future expectation of good are based on God's promise, not on how well you keep the Law of Moses?

_____

_____

_____

_____

The purpose of the Law (3:19-25)

The obvious question is, "If the Law wasn't given as a condition for attaining God's favor, then why was it given?"

Transgressions (3:19). Paul "has in mind intentional faults . . . the word used means a stepping aside from a right track. The law had laid down the right track and had made men conscious of deviations from it."[2]

---

7. List the things you find in 3:19-25 that the Law can and cannot do.

can	cannot

Mediator (3:19). Moses (see Exodus 19:7-9).

8. What did Moses do as the mediator between God and Israel (see Exodus 19:7-9)?

_____

_____

_____

_____

9. Where did this leave the ordinary person (see Exodus 19:20-22)?

DISCONNECTED

_____

_____

_____

God is one (3:20). The covenant through Moses
was two-sided and conditional: God promised
to do certain things if Israel did certain things.
A two-sided covenant requires a mediator. By
contrast, God's covenant with Abraham was
a one-sided and unconditional promise that
God would do certain things no matter what
anybody did. Since God is one party, He did not
need a mediator to make that covenant.

10. In this chart (which continues on page 72),
compare and contrast the giving of the Law
(3:19-20) with the giving of the promise
(verses 16 and 18).

Similarities

Law	promise

Differences

Law	promise

Sin (3:22). Our state of inner corruption makes it impossible for any law to make us righteous.

---

11. Why did you have to be a prisoner, confined by sin and by the Law, before you could receive what was promised through Jesus Christ?

_____

_____

_____

_____

_____

_____

Our guardian . . . under a guardian (3:24-25). A clearer translation might be, "The Law was our *custodian* until Christ came, that we might be justified by faith. But now that faith has come, we are no longer under a *custodian*" (3:24-25, RSV). The custodian (Greek: *paidagogos*) was "the personal slave-attendant who accompanied a freeborn boy wherever he went and exercised a certain amount of discipline over him. His function was more like that of a babysitter than a teacher."[3] "The discipline which he exercised was often of a severe character, so that those placed under his guardianship would yearn for the day of freedom."[4]

For Thought and Discussion: All Scripture is profitable for our growth (see 2 Timothy 3:16-17). What can you expect to gain from Old Testament Law?

Your response

12. Summarize in your own words what the Law did for people before the coming of Christ.

_____

_____

_____

_____

13. Fill in "Inheritance from Father" on the Alternatives in Galatians chart on page 33.

14. How is 3:15-25 relevant to your life?

_____

_____

_____

_____

15. What active response can you make to this truth this week?

_____

73

_____

_____

_____

16. List any questions you have about 3:15-25.

_____

_____

_____

_____

For the group

Warm-up. Ask each person to name one promise of God that is especially important to him or her.

Questions. The clearest understanding of truth often comes from sharing real-life experiences of it. Invite group members to share how they have been wrestling with the truths of Galatians, or how those insights have been affecting the way they live.

Explore the analogy of the legal agreement. Has anyone in the group experienced being held to a contract? Has anyone faced having someone else break a promise or agreement? Do any of you fear that God might break His word? What reasons do you have for being confident that He won't?

To understand relationship based on promise, you can ask your group, "Think of a relationship you have with someone else. Is your friendship, marriage, or parent-child commitment based on rules you must each follow or the relationship is dissolved? Or have you made promises you must keep regardless of how the other person acts?" Give each person a chance to name the relationship and state how he or she sees the terms of that relationship. Are your relationships based on promise or on law?

Try to come to some conclusions about what the Law is and isn't meant to accomplish. Then examine your own lives: Are you living by law or promise?

Prayer. Thank God that His promises to you are irrevocable. Thank Him for His Law that guided and protected you until you were ready for freedom in Christ. Thank Him for that freedom. Ask Him to help you to live joyfully in the security of freedom and promise.

1. For a more detailed discussion, see Donald Guthrie, *Galatians* (Grand Rapids, MI: Eerdmans, 1973), 101.
2. Guthrie, 104.
3. Kenneth Barker, ed., *The NIV Study Bible* (Grand Rapids, MI: Zondervan, 1985), 1784.
4. William Hendriksen, *Exposition of Galatians* (Grand Rapids, MI: Baker, 1968), 92. See also Alfred Edersheim, *The Life and Times of Jesus the Messiah*, one-volume ed. (Grand Rapids, MI: Eerdmans, 1971), 148.

GALATIANS 3:26–4:11

The Rights of a Son

It is not Paul's normal style to jump to a completely unrelated thought. Usually one idea leads into another, which leads into the next. In fact, since the earliest Greek manuscripts were written in uppercase letters with practically no punctuation, translators even have difficulty determining where to end Paul's sentences.

For this reason, a passage is best understood by reviewing what precedes it. For instance, Paul's comments about blessings received by faith (see 3:2-5) cause him to use Abraham as an example (see verse 6). So then, he writes about those who follow Abraham's example. They share in the promise God made to Abraham (see verses 7-9). By the time Paul devotes a paragraph specifically to promise (see verses 15-18), we can have a very clear idea of what he is talking about.

Reread chapter 3, paying special attention to references to "covenant" (will), "heir," "inheritance," "promise," and other mention of what God gives to us. Continue reading through 4:11.

1. How would you summarize Paul's main point in 3:26–4:11?

   _____

   _____

   _____

   _____

   _____

Optional Application: As you dress each day this week, remember that you have been clothed with Christ. You have come of age — God has empowered you to live by faith as a mature son or daughter! How can this affect your day?

2. Why are the promises and blessings through Abraham (see 3:6-18) important for understanding 3:26–4:11?

_____

_____

_____

_____

_____

_____

_____

3. How does the purpose of the Law (see 3:19-25) fit into 3:26–4:11?

_____

_____

_____

_____

_____

_____

Status with God (3:26-29)

Baptized into Christ (3:27). The rite of water baptism depicted the believer's immersion into Christ. To be baptized into Christ is to be united with Him and His body, the church. It is also to receive His Spirit (see Romans 6:3-11; 1 Corinthians 12:13).

Clothed yourselves with Christ (3:27). Paul may have been thinking of the Roman ceremony in which the toga of an adult was placed on a young man to declare that he had come of age.

4. How does being baptized into (united with) Christ affect your relationship to . . .

Christ's Father (3:26)? _____

_____

_____

_____

others who have been baptized into Christ (verses 27-28)? _____

_____

_____

_____

the promises God gave Abraham (3:29)?

_____

_____

_____

_____

5. In verse 29, Paul says that all who belong to Christ are Abraham's seed. Yet in 3:16, he made a point of Christ being the singular seed. In light of 3:27-28, how do you reconcile these two uses of seed?

_____

_____

_____

_____

_____

_____

_____

_____

For Thought and Discussion:
a. How do you reconcile the oneness and equality seen in 3:28 with other passages, such as Ephesians 5:22-24 and 1 Timothy 2:11-12, that emphasize differences?
b. What place do roles and distinctions have in Christian life, and what place do they not have (consider Luke 20:34-36; 1 Corinthians 7:17-24; Ephesians 6:5-9; 1 Timothy 6:1-2; 1 Peter 2:13-17)?

a. What do the mature son and the immature son have in common?

b. What do the immature son and the slave have in common?

Coming of age (4:1-7)

6. In 3:26–4:11, Paul distinguishes between three categories that people fall into. What are the traits of each group?

son with full rights	immature child	true slave
the spiritual state this represents		
relationship to Abraham		
relationship to inheritance		

Basic principles (4:3,9). "The Greek term meant essentially 'things placed side by side in a row' (as the ABCs) and then came to mean fundamental principles or basic elements of various kinds. The context here suggests that it refers to the elemental forms of religion, whether those of the Jews . . . or those of the Gentiles."[1] Both groups had sacrifices, rituals, and rites of external cleanliness to approach "holy" gods.

Time had fully come (4:4). God carefully timed the sending of His Son. The world scene was set for the spread of the gospel. Roman law and roads made travel commonplace. Roman currency and Greek language communicated clearly throughout most of the known world. Large urban centers served as hubs for the economic life of the Empire as well as for the spread of the gospel.

Pagan gods were losing their credibility. Slavery, sensuality, and luxury had produced a moral vacuum. The Jews were in bondage to Rome and messianic hopes were high. The dispersion of Jews, often with synagogues scattered throughout the world, gave a natural starting point for preaching and hospitality. Daniel's prophecy of weeks clearly pointed to the time God chose.

Yet what seems foremost in Paul's mind here is that years of bondage to rules and regulations had crushed all hope of fleshly release. Man was locked up in his own sin and condemned by every standard he tried to meet. Law had achieved its work.

---

7. Why do you think it was necessary for Christ to be born so completely entangled into the human situation (4:4; see also 2 Corinthians 5:21; Galatians 3:13)?

_____

_____

_____

_____

_____

_____

_____

Adoption to sonship (4:5). Under Roman law, a child was not a full son until he came of age. When he reached the age set by his father, the father formally adopted him as his heir. At that

For Thought and Discussion: Consider some of the other types of relationships that God could have chosen to have with us, rather than Father-son or Father-daughter. What differences would there have been if He had chosen to be an indifferent monarch, a harsh master, and so on?

For Thought and Discussion: To be God's sons and daughters, we need divine standing and capabilities. How do Christ and the Holy Spirit make our sonship possible? What does this tell you about what sonship really is?

For Thought and Discussion: At what point would calling God "Abba" become too presumptuous? Would living by human effort be more presumptuous or less? Why?

For Thought and Discussion: Sonship affects how we view ourselves and how we operate. In business, for example, how would the son of the owner behave differently from other employees?

point he received his full right to his authority and inheritance as a son.

8. What is the Spirit's function in regard to sonship (4:6-7; see also Romans 8:15-17; Ephesians 1:13-14)?

_____

_____

_____

_____

_____

_____

Abba, Father (4:6). The Aramaic word for Father, coupled with its translation. (Aramaic was the international language of the Babylonian Empire, so it became the native language of the Jews from the time of their exile to Babylon onward.) *Abba* was "the domestic term by which a father was called in the affectionate intimacy of the family circle."[2] It was thus roughly equivalent to "Papa" or "Dad." Such familiar address of God was not practiced by the Jews, but rather instigated by Jesus (see Mark 14:36).

---

9. What difference does it make to you that you can approach God as a mature son approaches a loving father?

_____

_____

_____

_____

_____

_____

Return to bondage (4:8-11)

10. a. What would be the difference between the Galatians' original slavery to pagan gods (4:8) and their return to slavery (4:9)?

_____

_____

_____

_____

_____

b. What would be the same?

_____

_____

_____

_____

_____

11. Why is the distinction between "knowing God" and "being known by God" (4:9) important?

_____

_____

_____

_____

_____

12. The pagan gods had their "weak and miserable principles," as did Judaism. What kinds of elementary rules and regulations could a Christian today put himself or herself in bondage to?

_____

_____

_____

_____

For Thought and Discussion: How do you think God feels when we try to approach Him on the basis of the rules we've kept as slaves, rather than with the loving confidence of sons and daughters?

For Further Study: Read Jesus' parables about the son who acted like a slave (see Luke 15:25-32). Note especially verse 29. Do you have this attitude deep down?

13. Why would a person choose to live as a slave keeping rules rather than have to relate to God as a son or daughter?

_____

_____

_____

_____

_____

Your response

14. Fill in "Relationship to God" on the Alternatives in Galatians chart on page 33.

15. What truth in 3:26–4:11 stands out to you as something you want to apply to your life?

_____

_____

_____

_____

16. How can you put this truth into practice this week?

_____

_____

_____

_____

17. List any questions you have about 3:26–4:11.

_____

_____

_____

_____

_____

_____

For the group

Warm-up. Ask, "What would it mean to have the rights of a king's son?"

Questions. Focus on what it means to be God's sons. (In that culture, daughters did not have the same rights as sons, but 3:28 makes it clear that Christian women also have the rights of God's sons.) Many Christians have trouble seeing themselves as God's sons and daughters, so they settle for acting like His slaves. Explore why this is foolish. Some of the optional questions may help.

Many people are raised on the principle that "If I do right, Mommy and Daddy will love me, but if I'm bad, they won't." Such an upbringing makes it hard for them to break the lie that "If I do right, my heavenly Daddy will love me, but if I'm bad, He won't." Ask group members whether their parents raised them to earn approval, or whether they were loved no matter what. Plan to pray for those who feel that their upbringing is getting in the way of their acting like free sons and daughters of their heavenly Dad.

Prayer. Thank your Father for making you His dear sons and daughters rather than His slaves. Thank Him for sending His Son to free you from slavery to rules, and for sending His Spirit to assure you that you are free. Ask Him to help each of you believe deep down that He loves you just for yourselves, regardless of how well you keep the rules.

1. Kenneth Barker, ed., *The NIV Study Bible* (Grand Rapids, MI: Zondervan, 1985), 1785.
2. F. F. Bruce, *The Epistle to the Galatians* (Grand Rapids, MI: Eerdmans, 1982), 199.

GALATIANS 4:12-31
A Choice of Allegiance

Paul spends more than 70 percent of this letter on historical and theological matters, arguing for the truth from which the Galatians were being drawn away. Maybe you are asking, *When will he get to the practical stuff?*

Well, not quite yet. The focus on daily living will come after he brings his readers to a point of decision. Paul is beginning to make an appeal for a decisive return to truth.

Read 4:12-31 twice, as well as 5:1, which Paul will use as his springboard into the next section.

Paul's personal plea (4:12-19)

1. a. What do you sense is Paul's mood at this point?

_____

_____

_____

b. What does this tell you about him?

_____

_____

_____

_____

Optional Application: How is Paul an example for you in ministry toward others?

For Thought and Discussion: Why do you think Paul brings up the matter of his illness?

For Further Study:
a. Why do you think God allowed Paul to suffer so? How could he minister when he had such problems? Look for answers in 2 Corinthians 4:7-12 and 2 Corinthians 12:7-10.
b. Do personal hardships shut down or strengthen your ministry to others?

2. Read 1 Corinthians 9:20-23 in light of Galatians 1:13-14. In what ways did Paul "become like" the Galatians (4:12)?

_____

_____

_____

_____

_____

3. In what ways did Paul want the Galatians to become like him?

_____

_____

_____

_____

Illness (4:13-14). The Bible gives no clear indication of what this illness was. Verse 15 implies to some readers that it was an eye problem, while others suggest epilepsy or malaria. Paul's illness either prompted a detour to their area or detained him in their area while traveling through.

4. What do you think the Galatians saw in Paul that they received him so eagerly?

_____

_____

_____

_____

_____

5. What differences do you see between Paul and the teachers who came later?

_____

_____

_____

_____

6. How did the Galatians lose their joy (4:15)?

_____

_____

_____

_____

For Thought and Discussion: What is Paul trying to say to the Galatians by comparing himself to a mother giving birth (see 4:19)?

Optional Application:
a. How full of joy are you?
b. What explanation and solution for the loss of joy does 4:15-16 suggest? Is it relevant to you? If so, how?

An allegory (4:21-31)

Law . . . the law (4:21). In the first instance, Paul is speaking of law in general, a system of established rules and regulations. In the second, he adds the definite article. *The* Law refers to the first five books of the Old Testament (see Matthew 7:12), because they contain the body of instructions that make up the Mosaic Law. Genesis was written by Moses and is included in the Law, even though its events occurred before God gave the Law at Mount Sinai.

7. What do you think is Paul's strategy in appealing to the Law in 4:21?

_____

_____

_____

_____

89

Family Tree
(Genesis 16:1-4; Genesis 21:1-5)

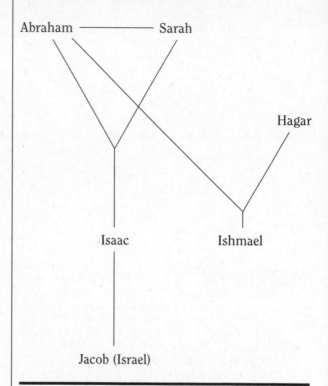

These things are being taken figuratively (4:24).
In an *allegory*, the earlier event has features
that correspond to a different situation. This
"presupposes that salvation-history displays a
recurring pattern of divine action."[1] For example, the Passover lamb corresponds to God's
later work in Christ.

Paul's method of interpretation here should
not be equated with mystical allegorization
that seeks hidden meanings and ignores the
historical facts of Scripture. Paul assumes that
the historical account is primary, and that the
lessons he sees should be apparent to others
as well (see 4:21). Paul also avoids pressing the
similarities between two events to a fanciful
extreme, either by drawing unwarranted conclusions or by giving each detail of the original
event a symbolic meaning.

8. a. Read the historical account behind Paul's allegory in Genesis 16:1-4 and Genesis 21:1-13. What was remarkable about the circumstances surrounding Isaac's birth that was not true of Ishmael's?

_____

_____

_____

_____

b. Why did conflict come about with Abraham's other son?

_____

_____

_____

_____

c. Why do you think Abraham was reluctant to send Ishmael and Hagar away?

_____

_____

_____

_____

d. Why did God say it was right?

_____

_____

_____

_____

For Thought and Discussion:
a. Why couldn't both Ishmael and Isaac have gotten along together?
b. What makes the law and freedom in Christ mutually exclusive?

Optional Application: What are some "Ishmaels" in your life — these things that keep you from living out God's promises to you? Purpose to eliminate them, even though they are as dear to you as sons, because they are interfering with what God wants to do in your life.

9. Complete the following chart by placing items from 4:21-31 in the correct spaces. Be especially alert to parallels between the left and right columns. Put an H by each person, place, or event that is part of the historical narrative of Abraham. Put an F by the figures that Paul says correspond to them. See the examples in the first box.

Sarah = *the free woman (H)* *heavenly Jerusalem (F)*	Hagar =

Isaac =	Ishmael =

From Mount Sinai (4:24). God gave the Law to Israel on Mount Sinai (see Exodus 19:1-8). Exodus 19:5 summarizes the "if . . . then" terms of that covenant.

Jerusalem (4:25-26). The earthly city of Jerusalem was the center of Jewish religion and government. Paul may be referring to its bondage under Rome as a picture of bondage to the Law that Christ had superceded (see 3:23-25). The Christian's worship and service are no longer directed to an earthly temple, but to the heavenly presence of God. Christ has given us access to God's throne room through a better covenant (see Hebrews 12:22-24).

10. a. Where does Paul put the Galatians on the chart in question 9?

_____

b. Where does he put the Judaizers who were troubling them?

_____

11. The Galatians were trying to live by both covenants. Why wouldn't that be possible?

_____

_____

_____

_____

12. In conclusion, what was Paul telling the Galatians to do (see 4:30)? Explain in your own words.

_____

_____

_____

_____

Your response

13. Add "Jewish Customs & Law" to the Alternatives in Galatians chart on page 33.

14. How is 4:12-31 relevant to your life?

_____

_____

_____

_____

15. What can you do to act on the implications of this passage?

_____

_____

_____

_____

16. List any questions you have about 4:12-31.

_____

_____

_____

_____

For the group

Warm-up. Ask, "Has thinking of yourself as a son or daughter of the King affected your life in any way this week? If so, how?"

Questions. One responsibility of a group is to model for one another. Enthusiasm is "easier caught than taught," but fear and criticism are catching, too. How well is your group doing during its time together at living in faith (see 2:20), in the Spirit (see 3:5), in sonship (see 4:6), and in joy (see 4:15)? In your prayer time, review the promises that God has granted to His children. Express your praise and dependence to Him.

We often think of sin as "enslaving." What about such good things as prayer notebooks, daily routines, church structures, and devotional guides? When would they become mere "human effort" (see 3:3)? What is and is not their proper place and use?

Prayer. Thank God that you are sons of the free woman, children of promise, and citizens of the heavenly Jerusalem. Ask Him to show you how to get rid of the slave woman and her son from your lives.

1. F. F. Bruce, *The Epistle to the Galatians* (Grand Rapids, MI: Eerdmans, 1982), 217.

GALATIANS 5:1-15
Christian Freedom

Reflect for a bit on where Paul has taken his readers so far. Do you suppose the Galatians are shocked by his sternness and awakened to the seriousness of their defection from the truth? For the rest of his letter, Paul shifts from persuasion to instruction, from the theological basis to the practical outworking. Read 5:1-15 twice.

Standing for freedom (5:1-6)

1. The first part of 5:1 seems almost too obvious to require saying. What is Paul's point?

_____

_____

_____

_____

_____

2. What pressures would the Galatians have to resist in order to "stand firm" (5:1)?

_____

_____

_____

_____

For Thought and Discussion:
a. What symptoms would you look for to see if another believer was being enslaved by rules and regulations?
b. What would you tell him to convince him of his error?

97

_____

_____

3. a. What does Paul say are the consequences if
the Galatians let themselves be circumcised
(see 5:2-3)?

_____

_____

_____

_____

b. Why are these consequences inevitable (see
5:4)?

_____

_____

_____

_____

_____

Alienated from Christ . . . fallen away from grace
(5:4). Seeking righteousness by law makes it
impossible to gain it through Christ. Some
readers see salvation at stake here, while others
see growth in righteous character as the issue.

The righteousness for which we hope (5:5). God's
final verdict of "not guilty" at the Last Judg-
ment. We can be confident of that final verdict
because of our faith and the Holy Spirit's ongo-
ing work of making our character more and
more like Christ's.

4. Paul identifies the essential criterion for being
right with God in 5:6. How would you distinguish real saving faith from a purely intellectual
faith?

_____

_____

_____

_____

_____

For Thought and Discussion:
   a. What things didn't Paul know about the Galatians' troublers?
   b. What did he know?

Repudiating error (5:7-12)

5. a. List some principles from 5:7-12 about how error gets into a group of believers.

_____

_____

_____

_____

_____

For Further Study:
Look at the figure of yeast in 1 Corinthians 5:6-12 and Matthew 13:33 and 16:11-12. Use an encyclopedia, dictionary, or cookbook to better understand how yeast works. What does yeast symbolize in each of these references and in Galatians 5:9?

b. In your own words, explain how to deal with such error (4:30; 5:1,13).

_____

_____

_____

_____

_____

_____

Preaching circumcision (5:11). Paul himself had apparently been misquoted as endorsing circumcision. This may have been because he circumcised Timothy, a disciple from Galatia. Timothy's mother was a Jew, but his father was a Greek. To the Greeks Timothy was a Jew, but to the Jews he was a Gentile. In order to make

For Further Study:
Paul discusses his
own freedom in
1 Corinthians 6:12; 8:9;
9:12,19-23. What prin-
ciples do you find for
your use of freedom?

Timothy's identity clear so that he could join Paul's ministry team, Paul circumcised him (Acts 16:1-3; 1 Corinthians 9:20). However, Paul refused to circumcise Titus, a full Greek, because his identity was already clear (Galatians 2:3).

Emasculate themselves (5:12). Paul is making a play on words by wishing that circumcision (literally a "cutting around") would extend to a total chopping off. His sarcasm may also imply a desire that the false teachers cut themselves off from the Galatian believers.

6. Why would requiring circumcision abolish the offense of the Cross (5:11)?

_____

_____

_____

_____

_____

Using freedom (5:13-15)

7. From your understanding of Paul's letter so far, how would you define "freedom"? (See 2:4 and note on freedom on page 40, if necessary.)

_____

_____

_____

_____

8. a. Do you value your freedom from sin and rules? If so, why?

_____

_____

_____

_____

_____

b. How do you show that you value your freedom? Describe at least one way.

_____

_____

_____

_____

_____

_____

Optional Application: List several people God has placed in your life. What can you do to serve them in love? Choose at least one need you can minister to this week.

The flesh (5:13). "Not what clothes our bony skeleton, but our fallen human nature, which we inherited from our parents and they inherited from theirs, and which is twisted with self-centeredness and therefore prone to sin."[1]

9. How is your Christian freedom different from the freedom your sinful nature and the world want you to claim (5:13)?

_____

_____

_____

_____

_____

10. a. What is Paul's guiding principle for freedom (5:13-14)?

_____

_____

_____

b. Why do you think this is such a good guideline?

_____

_____

_____

_____

11. List what for you would be some right and wrong uses of your freedom.

right	wrong

12. Paul uses a graphic figure of wild animals in an ugly struggle—"bite and devour each other" (5:15). Give an example to explain what you think Paul means by biting and devouring each other.

Optional Application: Identify relationships with fellow Christians that have been destructive. What changes does God want you to make in order to be constructive?

_____

_____

_____

_____

_____

Your response

13. Add "Use of Freedom" to the Alternatives in Galatians chart on page 33.

14. How would you summarize Paul's point in 5:1-15?

_____

_____

_____

_____

15. How is this (or some specific statement Paul makes) relevant to your life?

_____

_____

_____

_____

_____

16. What steps can you take this week to put what Paul says into practice?

_____

_____

_____

_____

_____

17. List any questions you have about 5:1-15.

_____

_____

_____

_____

_____

For the group

Warm-up. Take a few minutes to let members share how their efforts to apply Paul's words are going. Success? Frustration? Draw out some specifics. Then ask if they feel they are struggling to obey with human effort or learning to live by God's Spirit. Invite any questions about how to do the latter in specific situations, and see if the group can offer any help.

Questions. Make sure that each person has an honest chance to contribute to the group. Having different people share insights increases their sense of responsibility and worth. This will also help ensure that each person understands the key issues of the lesson. Even misdirected efforts can provide an occasion for learning.

Explore together what freedom means. Why is freedom so important to God that a return to the bondage of law alienates us from Him? What is the connection between salvation and freedom? How can you act with freedom in the specific circumstances you each are facing?

On the other hand, what prevents a connection between freedom and sin? Why should freedom lead to love and fulfilling God's moral Law? Will love ever lead a Christian to violate the Law if a situation seems to demand it? Why or why not?

Prayer. Thank God for setting you free from the slavery of law and sin. Ask Him for the grace of His Spirit to stand firm against the temptation to rely on rule keeping. Also ask for guidance on how to use your freedom to express your faith by serving others in love. Pray for ways to serve each other in love.

1. John R. W. Stott, *The Message of Galatians: Only One Way* (Downers Grove, IL: InterVarsity, 1968), 140.

GALATIANS 5:16-26

Living by the Spirit

If the Galatians thought Paul was saying that freedom in Christ meant license to do whatever they pleased, chapter 5 is undeceiving them. Circumcision is irrelevant to saving faith; love is not. But is love a new law to be kept by human effort? Read 5:16-26 several times, using different versions of the Bible if possible.

1. What do you see as the main teaching of this passage?

   _____

   _____

   _____

   _____

   _____

2. How is this passage related to 5:1-15?

   _____

   _____

   _____

   _____

   _____

   _____

For Thought and Discussion: How does the Spirit express His desires to us? How do you know if an internal prompting is from the Spirit of God or just your own thoughts?

A conflict (5:16-18)

It is sometimes easier to understand a difficult concept if we look at its opposite and work from the known to the unknown. Paul uses this technique in 5:16-26. We understand what it means to live by our sinful natures (flesh), so Paul uses this known experience to show what it means to live by the Spirit.

3. From your own experience, describe what it means to live by the desires of the sinful nature.

_____

_____

_____

_____

_____

4. Now by contrast, explain what you think it means to live by the Spirit. (*Optional:* See Romans 8:5-14.)

_____

_____

_____

_____

_____

5. Why is a person not "under law" if he or she is "led by the Spirit" (5:18)?

_____

_____

_____

_____

_____

Acts of the sinful nature (5:19-21)

Optional Application: Keep track for a day of all the things God's Spirit convicts you about and all the things He leads you to do. How do your lists compare with 5:19-23? This experiment should make you more attentive to the Spirit and less preoccupied with the sinful nature.

Study Skill — Word Definition

Knowing the meaning of words is the first step to understanding Scripture. Even looking up a word you assume you understand is often productive. You gain additional insight and correct misconceptions. In lists such as 5:19-23, defining words is the major direction of study.

Dictionaries are your primary tools. An English dictionary clarifies the precise meanings of words in an English translation of the Bible. A Bible dictionary includes most significant Bible words, usually in the terminology of the KJV. If you study with a different translation, you can use a KJV to figure out what word to look up in the dictionary.

Some dictionaries refer to distinctions among words in the original Greek or Hebrew. If you want to know the original Greek or Hebrew of the word you are researching, *Strong's Exhaustive Concordance* and *Young's Analytical Concordance* both have systems to help you find this information.

6. Using suggestions from the above Study Skill, record the meanings of at least three words you have questions about in 5:19-21.

a. _____

_____

_____

_____

_____

b. _____

_____

_____

_____

_____

For Thought and Discussion:
a. Why do you think Paul adds the expression "and the like" (5:21)?
b. What are some similar things you would add to the list?

c. _____

7. a. Which sins from 5:19-21 do you think are most frequently tolerated among Christians today?

b. Why do you think they are considered less serious than the others? (Are they really less serious?)

Those who live like this (5:21). "Referring to habitual practice rather than an isolated lapse."[1] An immoral, sensual, idolatrous way of life was commonplace among the Gentiles.

Kingdom of God (5:21). "The kingdom of God for Paul lies in the future: it is the heritage of the people of God in the age to come, the resurrection age."[2] (See also 1 Corinthians 6:9-10; Ephesians

110

5:5.) In Acts 14:21-22 Paul told the Galatian believers of the tribulations of life that would precede their entrance into the Kingdom of God.

For Thought and Discussion: What part does human thought and effort play in producing the fruit of the Spirit? Is it right to say, "I really need to work on the fruit of the Spirit in my life"? Is it okay to come up with "Ten Rules for Joy"?

8. Read Paul's warning about these sinful deeds and one's eternal destiny (5:21). How do you harmonize this with his earlier statements that salvation and inheritance are given by grace and received by faith (2:16; 3:18; 5:6)?

_____

_____

_____

_____

_____

_____

Fruit of the Spirit (5:22-23)

9. Select two characteristics of the fruit Paul lists. Use a dictionary and/or cross-references, and record what you discover.

   a. _____

   _____

   _____

   _____

   _____

   b. _____

   _____

   _____

   _____

111

Optional Application: Are you provoking and envying anyone (see 5:26)? Examine your heart for conceit, repent of those fleshly attitudes, and ask God for the strength of His Spirit to reject them.

10. What does the metaphor of "fruit" in contrast to "acts" (5:19) tell you about the way these good traits become a part of your life? (*Optional:* See John 15:1-8.)

_____

_____

_____

_____

_____

11. Paul brings up the concept of "law" again in 5:23. What is his point to the legalistic Galatians?

_____

_____

_____

_____

_____

Conflict resolved (5:24-26)

12. What is Paul's solution to the conflict between the sinful nature and the Spirit (see 5:24-25)?

_____

_____

_____

_____

112

13. Use connecting lines to match each deed of the sinful nature with at least one characteristic of the fruit of the Spirit that is its opposite.

sexual immorality   love

impurity

debauchery   joy

idolatry

witchcraft   peace

hatred   patience

discord

jealousy   kindness

fits of rage
                                     goodness
selfish ambition

dissensions   faithfulness

envy
                                     gentleness
drunkenness

orgies
                                     self-control

14. Which of these pairs represents your greatest conflict currently? Describe the specific situation.

_____

_____

_____

_____

_____

Keep in step (5:25). "Walk" in NASB. "Signifies to walk in line, and is used metaphorically of walking in relation to others."[3]

For Thought and Discussion: What can a person do to counteract all the stimulation and attention the sinful nature gets?

Optional Application:
a. Describe a current situation in which the conflict of opposing desires is very real for you.
b. How can you live by (submit to the control of) the Spirit in this situation?

15. How would you explain the difference between living by the Spirit and keeping in step with the Spirit (see 5:25)?

_____

_____

_____

_____

_____

16. What is the connection between our walk with the Spirit and our walk with one another (see 5:25-26)?

_____

_____

_____

_____

17. What do you need to realize and do in order to apply the solution of question 12 to the conflict you described in question 14? (Make some specific plans.)

_____

_____

_____

_____

_____

18. Fill in "Direction for Life" on the Alternatives in Galatians chart on page 33.

19. List any questions you have about 5:16-26.

_____

_____

For the group

Warm-up. Ask each person to give an example of how he or she has exercised his or her freedom in Christ during the past week.

Questions. One valuable theme in this passage is the internal conflict between the sinful nature and the Spirit. Let group members describe some of their own struggles in this area. Explore some ways you can respond correctly.

A related topic is what it means to have the infinite God dwelling in us, and what it means in practical terms to live by the Spirit. In what specific ways can you each live out His desires in your lives?

A third issue is the relationship between internal and external conflict. Ask group members to honestly trace conflicts they have with other people back to their roots in the struggle between the sinful nature and the Spirit. What internal changes do you need to make to restore harmony with others?

Questions like these are personal; they ask you to reveal areas of yourselves that you would prefer others not to know. If your group resists that kind of honesty, talk about why. Is there a fear that other members will gossip or look down on you? Are you too proud to admit your sins? Try to deal with fears and pride as a group until you are able to reach some level of trust.

Prayer. Ask God to enable each of you to live by the Spirit in the specific areas you have discussed. Thank Him that His power is available to you in your conflicts.

1. John R. W. Stott, *The Message of Galatians: Only One Way* (Downers Grove, IL: InterVarsity, 1968), 148.
2. F. F. Bruce, *The Epistle to the Galatians* (Grand Rapids, MI: Eerdmans, 1982), 251.
3. W. E. Vine, *An Expository Dictionary of New Testament Words*, vol. 4 (Old Tappan, NJ: Revell, 1952), 195.

GALATIANS 6:1-10

Keeping on Track

[handwritten margin note:] WITHOUT COMPARING TO OTHERS —GAL. 6:4-5

[handwritten margin note:] NOT BE WORRY IN DOING GOOD —GAL. 6:9

In chapters 1 and 2 Paul argued for the truth of the gospel. In chapters 3 and 4 he argued against the false "gospel" of legalism. Chapter 5 presented the way of life of the person who lives by the true gospel. Read 6:1-10 several times prayerfully.

1. How does 6:1-10 fit into the overall plan of the book?

[handwritten:] WHAT WE SHOULD BE DOING

Upkeep of the body (6:1-6)

Restore (6:1). "The Greek for this verb is used elsewhere for setting bones, mending nets, or bringing factions together."[1]

2. Explain in your own words what 6:1-6 teaches you to do in the following situations:

117

For Thought and Discussion:

a. Do you find that erring brothers are confronted as often as necessary? Do you find this done with gentleness? Describe your experiences.

b. Why is it sometimes easier to overlook sin and allow it to continue?

c. How does one know if he or she is "spiritual" enough to restore another?

d. How can you distinguish between pickiness and the times when you should confront sin?

Someone else in the church is sinning.

_____

_____

_____

_____

_____

Someone else is experiencing difficulties.

_____

_____

_____

_____

_____

You feel you are doing better than most in your church.

DON'T COMPARE TO OTHERS BUT TAKE PRIDE IN YOUR OWN ACTIONS

_____

_____

Someone is sacrificing time and income to be your teacher.

_____

_____

_____

_____

_____

3. Knowing that the same root word underlies both "Spirit" and "spiritual," look for hints in chapter 5 about what it means to "walk in the spirit."

118

Describe a "spiritual" person.

_____

_____

_____

_____

_____

_____

4. Consider Paul's cautions about restoring a sinning brother. What could happen if you ignored these warnings?

"restore him gently" _____

_____

_____

_____

"watch yourself" _____

_____

_____

_____

_____

5. How does Paul's approach to dealing with sin differ from legalism?

_____

_____

_____

_____

6. Few people intentionally plan to fall into sin. How would you "watch yourself"?

For Further Study:
a. Matthew 18:15-20 and 1 Timothy 5:19-20 offer more guidelines for dealing with a sinning brother.
b. In 1 Corinthians 5:1-13 and 2 Thessalonians 3:6-15 Paul deals with how to treat a brother who rejects admonition.

Optional Application: If you are aware of a sin in a fellow Christian's life, decide what Galatians 6:1-5 would have you do, and how. Then do it.

119

Optional Application: Ask God to show you someone who is struggling to manage a heavy burden that you can help shoulder. You may need to consider carefully some sacrifices you can make without neglecting your own responsibilities.

For Further Study: Romans 12:3-6 and 2 Corinthians 10:12-18 offer further insight for a correct view of oneself (see 6:4).

7. Why do you think Paul warns against *temptation* rather than *sin* in 6:1?

Burdens . . . load (6:2,5). Verse 2 speaks of an unsought and oppressive burden, while verse 5 uses a word often used of a man's pack, a load he is designed to bear.[2]

8. Read John 13:34 and 15:12. Carefully state "the law of Christ" mentioned in Galatians 6:2.

9. How does Christ's example show you what it means for you to carry someone else's burden?

_____

10. What criteria would you use to "test [your] own actions" (6:4) in order to honestly evaluate yourself?

_____

_____

_____

_____

_____

_____

Planting for a harvest (6:7-10)

11. Describe at least one situation in your own life where you have seen 6:7 come true.

_____

_____

_____

_____

_____

12. Why do you think God's honor is at stake in these matters?

_____

_____

_____

_____

_____

For Thought and Discussion:
a. How do you tell if you should help someone or if they should handle it on their own?
b. Do you think you should help someone else before your own responsibilities are in order? Why or why not?

Optional Application: In light of 6:3-5, how are you doing at carrying your part of the church's responsibilities? How do you need to grow in this area?

For Further Study: Paul presents an extended case for the laborer in Christian ministry being worthy of wages in 1 Corinthians 9:3-18. Why did Paul preach this for others but not demand it for himself?

Optional Application: Take an inventory of where your time and resources are being planted. (You may want to select one category, such as "weekend time" or "personal expenses.") What areas do not reflect the harvest you want?

Optional Application: What opportunities do you have right now to "do good" (6:10)?

Optional Application: Do something each day to sow seeds of good. Don't be afraid to cover it up and wait for results. Keep a log and see what kind of a harvest results.

13. Surely everyone wants a good harvest. Why would anyone (including you) plant bad seed (consider 6:8-9)?

_____

_____

_____

_____

_____

14. Why do you think special emphasis should be given to doing good to believers (see 6:10)?

_____

_____

_____

_____

_____

Your response

15. Complete "Consequences of Actions" on the Alternatives in Galatians chart on page 33.

16. What stands out from 6:1-10 as something you want to take to heart?

_____

_____

_____

_____

_____

17. How would you like this to affect your life?

_____

_____

_____

_____

_____

18. What action can you take to put this into practice?

_____

_____

_____

_____

19. List any questions you have about 6:1-10.

_____

_____

_____

_____

For the group

Warm-up. Ask group members each to name a conflict between the sinful nature and the Spirit they have been experiencing. These will raise some ideas about how to bear each other's burdens.

Questions. Don't forget to follow up on earlier commitments people in the group have made. Most people need encouragement and prayer support to make changes in their way of life that stick. Also, members will be motivated to apply God's Word as they get excited about the growth in others. It's a good idea to check up briefly at each meeting on how earlier applications are going. You now have a basis for avoiding legalism when you discuss applications, so you can keep from driving each other to grow by human effort.

By bringing your group together on the issues Paul raises, you may be able to counter some of the pressure society exerts on your behavior. For instance, some strong cultural values work against dealing with a sinning brother, getting involved in someone else's difficulties, or spending your time and money on a future and spiritual harvest. What are some of those cultural values? What can you do as a group to help each other counter their influence?

Prayer. Pray for the burdens and conflicts between sinful nature and Spirit that members are experiencing. Ask God how you can sow into the Spirit. Ask Him for the strength to not grow weary in doing good, but to rejoice in the eternal harvest that awaits you.

1. Kenneth Barker, ed., *The NIV Study Bible* (Grand Rapids, MI: Zondervan, 1985), 1787.
2. J. B. Lightfoot, *St. Paul's Epistle to the Galatians*, 6th ed. (London: Macmillan, 1880), 217.

GALATIANS 6:11-18 AND REVIEW

Focusing on the Eternal

Paul now draws his exhortation to a point in these last few paragraphs. Read 6:11-18.

Large letters (6:11). Paul has apparently dictated the letter up to this point. Then, as is his normal custom, he ends with a personal greeting in his own hand (see 2 Thessalonians 3:17). The large letters may be in contrast to the neatness of the secretary or for emphasis. Some attribute them to poor eyesight.

1. What thoughts seem to be heaviest on Paul's heart as he makes his final comments?

_____

_____

_____

_____

_____

_____

The wrong reasons (6:12-13)

2. What reasons does Paul think are motivating those who are pushing circumcision on the Gentiles? (Explain in your own words.)

_____

_____

_____

_____

_____

3. How might Christians do things for similar motives today?

_____

_____

_____

_____

4. How would you guard yourself against each of these dangers in your own service for Christ?

_____

_____

_____

_____

The right reasons (6:14-17)

5. What would you say if you wanted to boast in the Cross of Christ (see 6:14)?

_____

_____

_____

_____

_____

6. a. Paul says that through the Cross, the world was crucified to him. How would it be possible to live as if the world was dead and gone?

_____

_____

_____

_____

_____

b. From the opposite viewpoint, why would Paul be dead as far as the world was concerned?

_____

_____

_____

_____

_____

Optional Application: How can you live as one who is crucified to the world?

Optional Application: Religious boasting may be the most subtle form of exalting oneself. Make a list of external criteria that symbolize your status with God. Cross each one off as you write down a work of Christ in your life that is even greater, maybe even contrary to what you tried to do.

Israel of God (6:16). In contrast to ethnic Israel. Paul is probably assuring the Galatians of their place in spiritual Israel (see 3:28-29). Some versions translate the phrase "also to the Israel of God," so that Paul is wishing peace upon believing Jews (Romans 9:6) who live by his rule of Galatians 6:15.

Marks (6:17). This word "was used of the brand that identified slaves or animals."[1] Paul's stoning, beating, illness, arduous travel, and short rations marked him as Christ's slave.

7. How can you live by the rule that Paul mentions in 6:15-16? Think of one practical way.

_____

_____

_____

127

For Further Study:
Paul keeps putting in little side comments about law (see 5:14,18,23; 6:2,13). How do each of these burst the law-conscious Galatians' desire to live by law?

_____

_____

Review

8. Summarize the basic problem the Galatians faced.

_____

_____

_____

_____

_____

9. Referring only to your Bible, state Paul's basic argument in each of these major sections.

1:10-24 _____

_____

_____

_____

2:1-10 _____

_____

_____

_____

2:11-21 _____

_____

_____

_____

V

3:1-14 _____

_____

_____

_____

_____

3:15-25 _____

_____

_____

_____

_____

3:26–4:11 _____

_____

_____

_____

_____

4:12-31 _____

_____

_____

_____

_____

10. Summarize the active response to this truth
that Paul urges in 5:1–6:18.

- serve each other in love
- live by the Spirit
- Restore brothers/sisters gently
- Do good to all
-

11. Review the questions you listed at the ends of lessons 1 through 11. Do any important ones remain unanswered? If so, some of the sources in Study Aids may help you answer some of them. Or, you might plan to study some particular passage with cross-references. Write down your unanswered questions.

_____

_____

_____

_____

_____

12. Have you noticed any areas (thoughts, attitudes, opinions, behavior) in which you have changed as a result of your study of Galatians? If so, how have you changed?

_____

_____

_____

_____

13. Look back over the entire study at questions in which you expressed a desire to make some specific application. Pray about any of those areas that you think you should continue to pursue specifically.

What topics continue to challenge you, and what do you plan to do about them?

_____

_____

_____

_____

- DOES MY LIFE REFLECT BEING FREE IN CHRIST

- WHAT IS ONE THING CHANGE TO MAKE SO THAT YOU ARE WALKING IN THE SPIRIT

_____

_____

_____

For the group

Questions. You probably don't need to spend a lot of time on 6:11-18. Concentrate on pulling together an overview of what Paul is saying in this letter, and on reviewing your efforts to put his words into practice. Give members a chance to voice any questions they still have about Galatians, and plan ways for them (not you, the leaders) to seek answers.

Evaluation. Take a few minutes or a whole meeting to assess how your group functioned during your study of Galatians. Some questions you might ask are:

How well did the study help you grasp Galatians?
What were the most important truths you learned
    together about the Lord?
What did you like best about your meetings?
What did you like least? What would you change?
How well did you meet the goals you set at your
    first meeting?
What did you learn about small group study?
What are members' current needs and interests?
What will you do next?

Prayer. Thank God for specific things He has taught you and specific ways He has changed you through Galatians. Thank Him also for the opportunity to study the Bible together. Pray for guidance about what to do next.

1. Kenneth Barker, ed., *The NIV Study Bible* (Grand Rapids, MI: Zondervan, 1985), 178.

131

STUDY AIDS

For further information on the material covered in this study, consider the following sources. If your local bookstore does not have them, you can ask the bookstore to order them from the publishers, or find them in a public university or seminary library. If they are out of print, you might be able to find them online.

Commentaries on Galatians

Bruce, F. F. *The Epistle to the Galatians* (New International Greek Testament Commentary, Eerdmans, 1982).
    Excellent introductory material. The commentary section is admirable too, but it is scholarly and technical, and a non-Greek reader would find it hard to follow.

Cole, R A. *The Epistle to the Galations* (Tyndale New Testament Commentaries, Eerdmans, 1971).
    A concise reference tool for those who don't know Greek. Cole focuses on the meaning of the text without delving into technicalities. The book is especially valuable for word definitions, and the Greek words are transliterated into the English alphabet.

Guthrie, Donald. *Galatians* (New Century Bible Commentary, Eerdmans, 1973).
    Excellent phrase-by-phrase explanation for the English reader. Guthrie gives an impartial and thorough presentation of conflicting views. Good background on the letter.

Hendriksen, William. *Exposition of Galatians* (Baker, 1968).
    A straightforward and thorough verse-by-verse exposition. Abundant in cross-references and biblical illustrations. Greek is confined to the footnotes.

MacArthur, John F. *Galatians* (Moody, 1987).

A very readable exposition that breathes of daily life. The phrase-by phrase consideration focuses on practical issues for English readers.

Stott, John R. W. *Only One Way: The Message of Galatians* (The Bible Speaks Today Series, InterVarsity, 1968).
A principle-by-principle analysis designed for personal growth. Stott clearly explains what the letter teaches and applies it to modern life.

Histories, concordances, dictionaries, and handbooks

A *history* or *survey* traces Israel's history from beginning to end, so that you can see where each biblical event fits. *A Survey of Israel's History* by Leon Wood (Zondervan, 1970) is a good basic introduction for laymen from a conservative viewpoint. Not critical or heavily learned, but not simplistic. Many other good surveys are also available. On the Persian period, serious students will enjoy *History of the Persian Empire* by A. T. Olmstead (University of Chicago, 1948). Also, Herodotus's *Histories* is available in English translation from several publishers.

A *concordance* lists words of the Bible alphabetically along with each verse in which the word appears. It lets you do your own word studies. An *exhaustive* concordance lists every word used in a given translation, while an *abridged* or *complete* concordance omits either some words, some occurrences of the word, or both.

Two of the three best exhaustive concordances are the venerable *Strong's Exhaustive Concordance* and *Young's Analytical Concordance to the Bible*. Both are available based on the King James Version and the New American Standard Bible. *Strong's* has an index in which you can find out which Greek or Hebrew word is used in a given English verse (although its information is occasionally outdated). *Young's* breaks up each English word it translates. Neither concordance requires knowledge of the original languages.

Perhaps the best exhaustive concordance currently on the market is *The NIV Exhaustive Concordance*. It features a Hebrew-to-English and a Greek-to-English lexicon (based on the eclectic text underlying the NIV), which are also keyed to *Strong's* numbering system.

Among other good, less expensive concordances, *Cruden's Complete Concordance* is keyed to the King James and Revised Versions, the *NIV Complete Concordance* is keyed to the New International Version. These include all references to every word included, but they omit "minor" words. They also lack indexes to the original languages.

A *Bible dictionary* or *Bible encyclopedia* alphabetically lists articles about people, places, doctrines, important words, customs, and geography of the Bible.
The New Bible Dictionary, edited by J. D. Douglas, F. F. Bruce, J. I. Packer, N. Hillyer, D. Guthrie, A. R. Millard, and D. J. Wiseman (Tyndale,

1982) is more comprehensive than most dictionaries. Its 1,300 pages include quantities of information along with excellent maps, charts, diagrams, and an index for cross-referencing.

Unger's Bible Dictionary by Merrill F. Unger (Moody, 1979) is equally good and is available in an inexpensive paperback edition.

The Zondervan Pictorial Encyclopedia edited by Merrill C. Tenney (Zondervan, 1975, 1976) is excellent and exhaustive, and has been revised and updated. Its five 1,000-page volumes represent a significant financial investment, however, and all but very serious students may prefer to use it at a church, public college, or seminary library.

Unlike a Bible dictionary in the above sense, *Vine's Expository Dictionary of New Testament Words* by W. E. Vine (various publishers) alphabetically lists major words used in the *King James Version* and defines each New Testament Greek word that the KJV translates with its English word. *Vine's* also lists verse references where that Greek word appears, so you can do your own cross-references and word studies without knowing any Greek.

Vine's is a good, basic book for beginners, but it is much less complete than other Greek helps for English speakers. More serious students might prefer *The New International Dictionary of New Testament Theology*, edited by Colin Brown (Zondervan) or *The Theological Dictionary of the New Testament* by Gerhard Kittel and Gerhard Friedrich, abridged in one volume by Geoffrey W. Bromiley (Eerdmans).

A **Bible atlas** can be a great aid to understanding what is going on in a book of the Bible and how geography affected events. Here are a few good choices.

The Macmillan Atlas by Yohanan Aharoni and Michael Avi-Yonah (Macmillan, 1968, 1977) contains 264 maps, 89 photos, and 12 graphics. The many maps of individual events portray battles, movements of people, and changes of boundaries in detail.

The New Bible Atlas by J. J. Bimson and J. P. Kane (Tyndale, 1985) has 73 maps, 34 photos, and 34 graphics. Its evangelical perspective, concise and helpful text, and excellent research make it a very good choice, but its greatest strength lies in outstanding graphics, such as cross-sections of the Dead Sea.

The Bible Mapbook by Simon Jenkins (Lion, 1984) is much shorter and less expensive than most other atlases, so it offers a good first taste of the usefulness of maps. It contains 91 simple maps, very little text, and 20 graphics.

The Moody Atlas of Bible Lands by Barry J. Beitzel (Moody, 1984) is scholarly, evangelical, and full of theological text, indexes, and references. This admirable reference work will be too deep and costly for some, but Beitzel shows vividly how God prepared the land of Israel perfectly for the acts of salvation He planned to accomplish in it.

A **handbook** of biblical customs can also be useful. Some good ones are *Today's Handbook of Bible Times and Customs* by William L. Coleman (Bethany, 1984) and the less detailed *Daily Life in Bible Times* (Nelson, 1982).

For small-group leaders

The Small Group Leader's Handbook by Steve Barker et al. (InterVarsity, 1982). Written by an InterVarsity small group with college students primarily in mind. It includes information on small group dynamics and how to lead in light of them, and many ideas for worship, building community, and outreach. It has a good chapter on doing inductive Bible study.

Getting Together: A Guide for Good Groups by Em Griffin (InterVarsity, 1982). Applies to all kinds of groups, not just Bible studies. From his own experience, Griffin draws deep insights into why people join groups; how people relate to each other; and principles of leadership, decision making, and discussions. It is fun to read, but its 229 pages will take more time than the above book.

You Can Start a Bible Study Group by Gladys Hunt (Harold Shaw, 1984) Builds on Hunt's thirty years of experience leading groups. This book is wonderfully focused on God's enabling. It is both clear and applicable for Bible study groups of all kinds.

How to Build a Small Groups Ministry by Neal F. McBride (NavPress, 1994) This hands-on workbook for pastors and lay leaders includes everything you need to know to develop a plan that fits your unique church. Through basic principles, case studies, and worksheets, McBride leads you through twelve logical steps for organizing and administering a small groups ministry.

How to Lead Small Groups by Neal F. McBride (NavPress, 1990). Covers leadership skills for all kinds of small groups—Bible study, fellowship, task, and support groups. Filled with step-by-step guidance and practical exercises to help you grasp the critical aspects of small group leadership and dynamics.

Bible study methods

Braga, James. *How to Study the Bible* (Multnomah, 1982). Clear chapters on a variety of approaches to Bible study: synthetic, geographical, cultural, historical, doctrinal, practical, and so on. Designed to help the ordinary person without seminary training to use these approaches.

Fee, Gordon, and Douglas Stuart. *How to Read the Bible for All Its Worth* (Zondervan, 1982). After explaining in general what interpretation and application are, Fee and Stuart offer chapters on interpreting and applying the different kinds of writing in the Bible: Epistles, Gospels, Old Testament Law, Old Testament narrative, the Prophets, Psalms, Wisdom, and Revelation.

Fee and Stuart also suggest good commentaries on each biblical book. They write as evangelical scholars who personally recognize Scripture as God's Word for their daily lives.

Jensen, Irving L. *Independent Bible Study* (Moody, 1963), and *Enjoy Your Bible* (Moody, 1962).
  The former is a comprehensive introduction to the inductive Bible study method, especially the use of synthetic charts. The latter is a simpler introduction to the subject.

Wald, Oletta. *The Joy of Discovery in Bible Study* (Augsburg, 1975).
  Wald focuses on issues such as how to observe all that is in a text, how to ask questions of a text, how to use grammar and passage structure to see the writer's point, and so on. Very helpful on these subjects.

Discover What the Bible Really Says

LifeChange by The Navigators

The LifeChange Bible study series can help you grow in Christlikeness through a life-changing encounter with God's Word. Discover what the Bible says—not what someone else thinks it says—and develop the skills and desire to dig even deeper into God's Word. Each study includes study aids and discussion questions.

LifeChange $9.99			
Genesis	9780891090694	1 Corinthians	9780891095590
Exodus	9780891092834	2 Corinthians	9780891099512
Joshua	9780891091219	Galatians	9780891095620
Ruth & Esther	9780891090748	Ephesians	9780891090540
1 Samuel	9780891092773	Philippians	9780891090724
1 & 2 Kings	9781615216413	Colossians & Philemon	9780891091196
Job	9781615216239	1 Thessalonians	9780891099321
Psalms	9781615211197	2 Thessalonians	9780891099925
Proverbs	9780891093480	1 Timothy	9780891099536
Isaiah	9780891091110	2 Timothy	9780891099956
Matthew	9780891099963	Titus	9780891099116
Mark	9780891099109	Hebrews	9780891092728
Luke	9780891099307	James	9780891091202
John	9780891092377	1 Peter	9780891090526
Acts	9780891091127	2 Peter & Jude	9780891099949
Romans	9780891090731	1, 2 & 3 John	9780891091141
		Revelation	9780891092735

Over 35 titles available. See a complete listing at NavPress.com.

To order copies, call NavPress at **1-800-366-7788** or log on to **www.NavPress.com**.

 Facebook.com/NavPressPublishing   Twitter.com/NavPress

NAVPRESS
Discipleship Inside Out™

BULK PRICING
Is Available
Order enough for everyone in your group!

Percentage discounts for bulk purchases of *single* items	
Quantity	**Discount %**
10-29	20%
30-49	25%
50-69	30%
70-99	35%
100-499	40%

(Discounts apply to retail prices)

Don't leave anyone out! NavPress offers bulk pricing on books, Bibles, and Bible studies.*

*Some exclusions apply.

For more information on all NavPress products or to find additional Bible studies, go to **www.NavPress.com** or call **1-800-366-7788**.

NAVPRESS

Discipleship Inside Out®